10 Things That Keep CEOs Awake

10 Things That Keep CEOs Awake

And How to Put Them to Bed

Elizabeth Coffey and colleagues
from The Change Partnership

THE McGRAW-HILL COMPANIES

London · Burr Ridge IL · New York · St Louis · San Francisco · Auckland
Bogotá · Caracas · Lisbon · Madrid · Mexico · Milan
Montreal · New Delhi · Panama · Paris · San Juan · São Paulo
Singapore · Sydney · Tokyo · Toronto

The McGraw·Hill Companies

10 Things that Keep CEOs Awake: And How to Put Them to Bed
Elizabeth Coffey & colleagues from The Change Partnership

0077099893

Published by McGraw-Hill Professional
Shoppenhangers Road
Maidenhead
Berkshire
SL6 2QL
Telephone: 44 (0) 1628 502 500
Fax: 44 (0) 1628 770 224
Website: www.mcgraw-hill.co.uk

British Library Cataloguing in Publication Data
A catalogue record for this book is available from the British Library

The Library of Congress data for this book is available from the Library
of Congress

Sponsoring Editor: Elizabeth Choules
Editorial Assistant: Sarah Butler
Business Marketing Manager: Elizabeth McKeever
Senior Production Manager: Max Elvey
Production Editor: Eleanor Hayes

Produced for McGraw-Hill by Gray Publishing, Tunbridge Wells
Text design by Robert Gray
Printed and bound in the UK by Clays Ltd, Bungay, Suffolk
Cover design by Simon Levy Associates

McGraw-Hill books are available at special quantity discounts. Please
contact the Corporate Sales Executive at the above address.

Contents

Contributors

Elizabeth Coffey

'A midwife is needed for ideas to be born. This Socratic view provides a vibrant model for coaching excellence.' Educated at Wellesley College, Elizabeth honed her research and counselling skills at Boston teaching hospitals before moving to Germany. There she co-founded a consultancy that designed and delivered cross-cultural development programmes. In London, at Saxton Bampfylde International Plc, she carried out director-level executive searches across many business sectors in the UK and world-wide. She advises Boards and lectures widely on diversity issues and leadership.

John Coleman

'Coaching is always dynamic and it's the results – always – which matter.' An Oxford graduate, John spent three decades at ICI in a wide range of roles with international responsibilities, encompassing manufacturing, sales and marketing, general management, environmental affairs and human resources. After four years heading the group's HR functions, he left ICI in 1996 to act on his belief in coaching as uniquely effective techniques for the personal development of senior people.

Geoffrey Dale

'The value in coaching over a longer period lies in the many opportunities to use work situations as learning points.' Commissioned in the Army, Geoffrey saw active service in Cyprus before going up to Oxford. After a Postgraduate Diploma in Public and Social Administration, he joined Cadbury as a graduate trainee. Following a series of key functional and line positions, and a Board position at Schweppes, he became Group HR Director for Cadbury Schweppes Plc.

Heather Dawson

'Coaching is a wonderful way to help senior executives think through how they will lead their organizations.' After graduating from business school in Canada, Heather worked in consumer goods marketing before a career in strategy consulting with McKinsey & Co. She then founded her own consulting practice in Canada. After 12 years in strategic consulting, she began coaching senior executives, and working with their senior management to help them develop strategic direction and leadership skills.

Sue Godfrey

'Working together as thought partners on your agenda, we will stimulate your ideas, grow your knowledge and contribution, and help you realize your full potential.' Sue has worked in a range of business sectors, including pharmaceuticals, automotive, facilities management and health care, and has developed executives in the very different business cultures in North America, Latin America, South-east Asia, Europe and the UK. Her career has focused on personal and organisational development in changing environments.

Bob Goodall

'I was an enthusiastic advocate of coaching, for both myself and my colleagues, during my corporate career.' Bob has spent his life in an international environment, including six years overseas with the United Nations and four years as the European HR Development Director for a major US pharmaceutical company. He had a number of years' experience as a Group HR Director for Inchcape, and, latterly, was Chairman of a public company in Singapore.

Robin Linnecar

'Working with unique people in a unique way each time gives me great satisfaction – helping clients understand how they can best use their skills and talents in the here and now to mutual

benefit is even more rewarding.' Robin Linnecar followed an English degree at Cambridge and chartered accountancy at Arthur Andersen with a wide range of senior HR roles at Shell, and as a partner in Deloittes, Coopers & Lybrand and KPMG.

Elspeth May

'You can achieve whatever you really want to.' Elspeth's career started in accountancy, and she became a partner in KPMG. As well as client responsibilities she had a number of in-house roles at various times, including HR and marketing. She also acted as the firm's spokeswoman on personal tax issues and handled the media. She has worked with many CEOs and gained considerable insight into the pressures and challenges they face.

Peter Milligan

'Success, happiness and confidence result from having a strong sense of purpose, a commitment to outcomes and the enjoyment of learning.' Born and educated in Australia, Peter worked as an IT consultant for several years, before training as an occupational psychologist and achieving a senior management role at Speakman Stillwell, a leading Australian HR consultancy. He was among the first in Australia to bring coaching into organizations.

Peter Salsbury

'Helping individuals discover their untapped potential and then make something of it is what matters most in my work.' Peter was the youngest member of the board of Marks & Spencer (as HR Director) before being appointed Managing Director and then CEO. A keen supporter of vocational education, he sits on the councils of City and Guilds and the Institute of Employment Studies. He is also a non-executive director of TR Property Investment Trust.

Peter Sedgwick

'Successful change is about you and your people. I believe in creating a unique space where individuals or groups can fully engage in the shift from ideas to action. This requires courage, pace, humour and imagination.' Peter began his career in architectural practice, before gaining an MBA and moving into senior roles at Sainsbury's. He then spent six years as a consultant at PricewaterhouseCoopers. He works alongside clients as a coach, group facilitator and change architect.

Peninah Thomson

'Real organizational transformation only happens when there is personal transformation in leaders.' Peninah's years as an international Civil Servant – undertaking assignments in 11 countries – grounded her in networking, diplomacy and negotiating. She moved into management consultancy and spent 11 years at PricewaterhouseCoopers, working with board members on strategy, organizational culture and leadership.

Preface

Simon Caulkin

For senior managers this is the best and worst of times. Now that the dust from the Internet bubble and Enron implosions has settled, the good news is that real business priorities have come into sharp focus again. We know that in the new economy people are as important as technology; that companies still have to earn more than they spend; and that shareholder value is created by selling products to satisfied customers, not by rearranging the balance sheet. For those that get these simple verities right, the outlook has never been brighter nor the opportunities greater.

The bad news is that actually doing it has never been harder. In themselves, decisions may or may not be too complicated; it is external pressures that make them 10 times harder to cope with. 'Events, dear boy, events,' said Harold Macmillan when asked what kept *him* awake at night. In the global, interconnected, always-on world that has evolved since the 1950s, the disruptive potential of 'events' – both inside and outside the organization – has multiplied many times over.

The consequence is that CEOs for much of the time are in the position of the snooker player or penalty taker facing a crucial play in the last seconds of the match. On the practice field, they would tuck the shot away 95 times out of 100. Doing the same in the glare of the television cameras with the eyes of millions on them, however, is an altogether different matter.

Stress, as Daniel Goleman has pointed out, makes people stupid. This is one reason why coaching's hour has come. A coach can't play the shot; but he or she can debate the angles – and more importantly by confirming the perspective help ensure that the play is true – in line with internal values – rather than fatally skewed by outside pressures.

Everyone plays lip service to teamwork. But it's my theory that the virtues of this kind of close, one-to-one partnership have long been neglected in business. Management and leadership are context-based, requiring different attributes in different circumstances. It's almost impossible for one person to cumulate all of them – leadership *and* meticulous administration, inspiration *and* reflection, bold adventure *and* judicious stewardship. Hence shortening CEO tenures as organizations juggle to meet ever-changing conditions. But although manifestly desirable, formal partnerships are rare at the top of organizations, all but ruled out by the cult of ego and heroic leadership which makes it hard for strong No 2s to be content with the job – or for CEOs to tolerate them. Coaching can supply much of this need without running foul of organizational politics.

The CEO's need for the support of a confidant, a sounding board, an impartial but engaged mentor, is greatly amplified by employment trends which have seen career responsibilities increasingly outsourced to the individual. Learning opportunities are fewer and less predictable in flatter hierarchies. Meanwhile research findings suggest that a depressing amount of management development, as usually understood, is wasted, usually because it can't be applied to the business. Being precisely both personal and grounded in the pressing demands of the job, coaching trumps these difficulties. In the future, coaching may come to be seen to be as inseparable from the attainment of full personal development in business, just as it is in sports.

And why not? Under the hype and hysteria – Kipling's twin impostors of 'disaster' and 'triumph' – management is a genuinely non-trivial pursuit. Uncomfortable as it may be, managers work daily at the intersection point of politics, economics and ethics where many of today's most important issues converge. Livelihoods, companies and communities – perhaps since 11 September even more than that – all depend on what they decide and how those decisions are carried out. In other words, it's in all our interests that managers should not only have steady nerves, but aim higher and consistently improve their strike rate. Raising their game is what coaching – and this book – is all about.

Foreword and Acknowledgements

Eight of the 10 chapters that follow include fictionalized scenarios. Two are case studies of innovative leadership development, in Glaxo Wellcome and the Civil Service, driven by the top men, Sir Richard Sykes and Sir Richard Wilson. All of them show how coaching intervention can be beneficial, and how the reader can use coaching techniques in tackling similar issues.

I thank my colleagues and co-authors for their support of this project, and their sterling work.

John Coleman has provided invaluable wisdom in content editing and has been a model of calm good humour throughout. My Executive Assistant, Kirsten Whiting, is, quite simply, a wonder! She has co-ordinated all the work for this book, answered (and usually anticipated) every query and request, smoothed ruffled feathers, and remained sweet-tempered and positive. Stephanie 'Slash-and-Burn' Lewis made sure that the editorial process remained fun.

I thank John Barker and Museji Takolia at the Cabinet Office and Sir Richard Sykes for permission to use their case studies; Elizabeth Choules of McGraw-Hill for commissioning the book; and Barbara Shore for her wonderful cartoons.

On a personal note, I must thank my son, Alexander, for putting up with his ever-busy mother and remaining a constant joy and credit to her. Our nanny and friend, Sonya, for keeping us sane even when my work/life balance doesn't allow for a life. Leila Abu Sharr, the indulgent friend who feeds and nurtures me without expecting reciprocity. The man in my life for much-needed spa breaks and for listening to me drone on about these '10 Things' when he has work concerns of his own. (I'm certainly the 11th thing for him!)

I dedicate this book to my father, Dr John J. Coffey, who taught me the art of coaching through Socratic questioning, and to my friend, Derek McKee, who inspires my ethnicity work.

Introduction

Peninah Thomson

This book covers territory familiar to all senior executives in the private sector – many of the topics will also have resonance for senior people in the public sector. Each chapter addresses an issue that looms large on the agenda of those leading national or global organizations, and the fictionalized examples, based on real coaching sessions with chief executive officers (CEOs), make it clear that leading an organization has never been more complex. The reasons for this are not hard to identify:

- the number and variety of stakeholders with a legitimate interest in the organization and very varied demands

- changing regulatory requirements

- technological advances

- changes in corporate governance

- a significant increase in the amount – and level – of risk now involved in leading a major enterprise.

The pressures are varied, as the book's chapter headings show. They range from the corporate and strategic (how to carve out the time to clarify the vision; retaining a hold on where one is actually taking the business; and managing the board), to the personal and intimate (thinking about how to retain some sort of balance between work and home).

Between the two poles of the strategic and the personal there are other challenges and dilemmas familiar to CEOs. Arguably more operational than strategic, but frequently no less demanding, they are everyday currency in their lives.

- Getting the right organizational structure, and deciding whether restructuring is *really* what is needed.

- Tussling with how best to run a global (and therefore multi-cultural) business.

- Creating appropriate organizational change.

- Acquiring, motivating, developing and keeping talented individuals.

- The never-ending task of communicating with stakeholders (all of them!).

Taken all in all these are, of course, within the compass of skills, qualities and attributes that most CEOs possess. Boards rarely appoint to top executive positions individuals whom they suspect do not have the ability to perform well in the role. What triggers insomnia in a CEO, what creates pressure and can place individuals under extreme stress, is often not a failure of ability *per se*, but the context in which they must perform. A context characterized by a relentless drive for bottom-line achievement in the short term, in an environment of constant strategic change in which the potential for failure is significant, coupled with high personal visibility and intense media interest. Combined, these features constitute a ferociously demanding working environment to which the man or woman at the top, to be successful, needs to bring an equally complex array of qualities and skills.

In the past decade, technology has been developed that enables instant communication and demands almost instant response, and globalization has led to a 24/7 mentality in the world business community. At the same time, industry convergence has led to increased competition, which now has to be met on a vast number of fronts, putting even more pressure on those at the top.

Before the business world started to operate at the frantic pace that is now the norm, organizations – especially large ones – tended systematically to develop a cadre of people from which their future leaders could be drawn. Individuals were developed for senior roles in the future by going on internal courses; studying at major business schools, often abroad; taking responsibility for business units overseas. Some were offered secondments to government to expose them to macro-economic policy making. This type of preparation for leadership roles was efficient, effective and appropriate. It still is, but it is no longer wholly adequate. CEOs' operating circumstances have changed and, consequently, new ways must be found to prepare top executives for the senior role and support them when they are in it.

It is difficult (and probably, ultimately, impossible) to establish causality in the circumstances driving business change. Arguably, it is shorter economic cycles that are driving companies and their leaders to achieve quicker returns. That trend in turn fuels the search for greater efficiencies, higher levels of innovation and increased productivity which, again, forces companies into many more interactions with a far wider group of stakeholders than was the case in the past. Those interactions may in themselves be a further source of pressure.

Whatever the causal links, though, it is clear that the prevailing pressure for high levels of shareholder return, driving the push for growth, places exceptional demands on senior people. In these circumstances a measured, essentially curriculum-based approach to top executive development is unlikely to provide contemporary CEOs with everything they need in terms of knowledge, skills, support, ideas, networks, creativity, counsel or comfort. Nor will learning from the experience of gurus or recently retired business leaders provide complete resolution to the dilemma of what, and how, to learn to keep ahead. The future is unlikely to look like the past, and the experience of great leaders of the past may be less applicable to emerging business conditions. Something more is needed urgently, because being at the top of an organisation is increasingly a short-term experience. The average tenure of a CEO in the USA is estimated to be just 18 months;[1] in the UK, at the moment, CEOs tend to stay for longer, around four years, but the trend is towards shortening.[2]

The 'something more' that is needed is, increasingly, a coach: someone who works in a supportive role alongside the chief executive. The common denominator in all the chapters that follow is the presence alongside the CEO of a coach, whose entire focus is to help enhance his (or, in one case, her) development as a leader and thus raise the performance of the organization he leads.

Executive coaching – widely used in the UK and USA, and in those countries where Anglo-Saxon management is the norm – is a personalized form of executive development. Good coaching is empirical, not theoretical: reality-driven, not case-study-driven; grounded in the client's daily experience of leading an organization. In the following coaching scenarios, chief executives share the substance of their daily working life to illuminate issues, drawing out the learning from actual events and real circumstances, albeit fictionalized here for confidentiality. By describing and reflecting upon what is 'in the field', and discussing unfolding events and potential outcomes with the coach, the chief executive develops insights and understanding that have immediate, and real, relevance and applicability.

A further characteristic of top-flight executive coaching is that it is essentially dialogue-based, and the dialogue focuses on personal learning on the part of the individual being coached. Coaches do not offer point solutions to problems or dilemmas, or expert consulting: they work to provide a safe, wholly confidential environment in which executives being coached can enhance their own learning, identify their own ways forward and arrive at their own solutions. Coaching is a *facilitative process* and, at its best, almost 'invisible'. In this book, however, we have made the coach visible so that the reader can see and subsequently use his or her techniques.

One of the essential benefits of an effective coaching process is that it demands reflection – something for which most CEOs have great difficulty ring-fencing the time. Often individuals leading organizations are in 'go' mode: dealing with an unending stream of decisions and issues that are – or are presented as being – both urgent and important. Responding to these can preclude CEOs from being able to think strategically about where they are taking the organization, with predictable results. One result of working with a coach, as this book makes plain, is an increased strategic focus.

As well as encouraging reflection, understanding and that 'helicopter view', effective coaches ensure that the dialogue focuses on outcomes: on action and results. They will attach great importance to every client making tangible progress in the achievement of his goal, whether that is a more bearable work/life balance, the successful conclusion of a major corporate action, or the resolution of difficult board dynamics.

There are several essential characteristics of a good coach, but perhaps the most obvious is discretion: the coach must be an unimpeachably confidential sounding board with whom the CEO can be open about every aspect of life. The coach must also be frank in turn: urging courage when the client is skittering away from confronting a difficult issue; holding up a metaphorical mirror to show how particular behaviours and approaches may be exacerbating a problem; challenging the thinking behind a particular course of action. And he or she must be a careful and intelligent listener: able to decode nuances of tone and vocabulary, speech and silence, in order to develop the client's thinking and elicit the best possible solutions to that client's specific challenges. The coach should be, in short, the embodiment of the adage that two heads are better than one.

Given the intensely personal nature of coaching, and the fact that the 'second head' will be very different in every coach–client relationship, it follows that the coaching is tailor made. One size does not fit all.

In this book the focus is necessarily on the 'story' told by the individual coach about the actual CEO who is its protagonist, the real issues faced, the means and manner through which those issues were addressed, and, finally, what happened – the outcomes.

The chapters that follow offer varied and valuable insights into the professional and personal lives of CEOs, and into the process and substance of coaching. Since this is, as its subtitle implies, in part a self-help book, each chapter concludes with a number of questions you could ask (and answer!) before tackling a similar situation.

This book is, in essence, about the fulfilment of potential. It is about the process of finding out who you are, envisioning what you have the potential to become, and shaping the journey that will take you to your future. The development of insight and awareness – which is at the heart of effective coaching – is at once supremely simple and very difficult: it occurs at its own pace and cannot be fudged. When it is developed, however, it is a solid and trustworthy foundation on which the individual can build.

> *'We shall not cease from exploration*
> *And the end of all our exploring*
> *Will be to arrive where we started*
> *And know the place for the first time.'*

T.S. Eliot, *Four Quartets*,
'Little Gidding' (1942)

*Hey, despite all of this he really **does** have a plan!*

Chapter 1

Developing Bifocal Vision

Heather Dawson

Context

The main responsibility of a chief executive officer (CEO) is to develop a clear vision of where he or she wishes to take the company and then to lead the company in that direction. (By 'vision', I mean the results that the CEO wishes to achieve.) Yet, I have found in my coaching practice that this is one area in which many CEOs have difficulty for three main reasons.

1. **CEOs have insufficient unallocated time to think and reflect.** Increasingly, CEOs of large organizations are being driven by the demands of the business: quarterly results, board meetings, executive committee meetings, meetings with analysts and key investors, annual strategy meetings and so on. Dealing with all these demands is essential, but senior executives can slip into the belief that this routine will provide the strategic direction for the company. Sometimes this rhythm can obscure the fact that the thinking, challenging, questioning and testing necessary for developing strategic direction are not taking place. The above-mentioned activities, and numerous others, leave little time for CEOs to reflect on where their businesses are going and to build their own skills for doing what is important, but not necessarily urgent.[1] Elspeth May examines how a CEO can create time in Chapter 3. Countless coaching clients voice real concerns that they have little time to breathe, or reflect about the business and how they should lead it.

2. **Retaining clarity for the short and long term is a rare skill.** People are often promoted into senior roles because of their

success in achieving annual revenue and profit targets, and many of them find it a big leap to managing performance for both the long and short term. Unfortunately, many executives whom I coach have not had the experience, formal training or apprenticeship time to learn this crucial skill. For some, the necessity to develop it comes as a rude shock. More importantly, there is constant pressure for short-term results. Senior executives are under enormous pressure to produce results quickly, with successive increases in revenue and profit. The pressure to sacrifice the long-term direction of the business for short-term successes is great. It takes courage to make decisions that resist this pressure. However, if the CEO knows what he or she wishes to achieve in the long run it is easier to place short-term decisions in context.

3. **CEOs must have all the answers.** The CEO is increasingly cast as the 'hero/heroine' for the company. He or she will be the individual who will 'save, restructure and turn around' the company, and be all things to all people! Not surprisingly, the average tenure of a CEO has dropped. At the same time, their remuneration has increased with the expectations. Investors and markets expect fast results. So, CEOs begin to feel that they must have all the answers. However, setting direction for a company requires input and help from several sources: employees, the board, the senior executives and sometimes, outside advisors. CEOs do not have the time, or often the skill, to do it alone. It is therefore crucial that they should develop their top team to help with the implementation of their vision.

In the maelstrom of running a company, how does a CEO retain focus on (and control of) operational issues, and chart its future direction?

This is not easy, and yet it is arguably the most crucial element of the CEO's job. Without a common direction and goals that are agreed by the senior executives, the CEO will not be around for very long. There are three useful skills that help CEOs retain clarity on where they wish to take the company.

1. **Balancing short and long term.** This is the skill both of creating and articulating a clear set of goals or results, and having a clear and dispassionate view of the company's current situation. This is a key focus of this chapter because so many executives often see their role with an 'either/or' perspective. The skill is balancing the two ends of the spectrum and articulating the path between the current reality of the company's situation and the goals for the business.

2. **Knowing when to be 'hands-off' and 'hands-on'.** This is the art of knowing how, and on what issues, a CEO should become involved. Many executives have learned or adopted a uniform approach for issues, whereas they need the ability to adapt their style to different situations if they are to achieve the best possible results. This can range from 'control freakery' to being so concerned with 'the big picture' that everything gets delegated. Many CEOs need to learn a flexible style of involvement so that they can spend their time more productively, including having more discretionary time for reflection and thinking on the company's direction, and building their own skills.

3. **Creating a strong senior executive group.** Without doubt every CEO needs a strong executive team that is clear on its mandate and has the skills to fulfil it. This well-functioning senior group will help the CEO enormously in developing goals and implementing plans to achieve them. Sue Godfrey covers another aspect of this in detail in Chapter 5.

This chapter describes the coaching programme for a CEO shortly after a difficult year for his company. Each of these three skills, with suggested frameworks, is highlighted and supported by illustrations from my work with him.

Client Company Profile

The company was a large multinational organization with a turnover of more than $2 billion, and over 8000 employees in Europe, Asia, and the United States. Throughout the 1990s the company recorded consistent profit and share growth. In 2000 it had suffered a sharp reversal in fortune because of rapid growth without sufficient operational controls and poorly performing investments outside its core businesses.

The company set about restoring profits and investor confidence by divesting quickly the loss-making acquisitions outside its core businesses, and replacing some of the senior management. I started to coach the CEO, Matthew, in 2001 as the business was stabilizing. The senior management changes had been completed and the board had approved the profit forecasts for the current and following fiscal years. Key investors were not happy with the company's performance, but for the moment, supported the plans to restore it.

Client Profile

Matthew was in his early 50s and had been the CEO for five years. He had been with the company for 12 years, and had risen through the ranks because of his deep experience and understanding of the business and its sector, natural leadership of people and innovative strategic expansion of the business. The board was clearly deeply concerned and unsettled by the sudden change in the company's performance in 2000. In spite of this they re-affirmed their confidence in Matthew because of his strategic skills, his knowledge of the core businesses and the support he had from senior management.

The Challenge

The core challenge for Matthew was to balance his priorities between stabilizing the business to meet short-term profit commitments and ensuring that the company was positioned for long-term growth. Matthew, inclined to focus on strategic projects and initiatives, recognized that he had to pay more attention to the operations of the core businesses. In the past, he had played to his strength of forging alliances and deals that had expanded the business globally and creating new ideas and concepts in business investment for his industry. Now, he risked losing the confidence of the board and key investors if he did not deliver on the upcoming fiscal year profit commitments and ensure that the alliances and deals delivered on expectations.

Not surprisingly, the board was putting pressure on him to focus mainly on the delivery of the short-term profit, but Matthew felt that he had to both deliver the profit commitments and review the strategic options. It was also important that he lead, more proactively, the senior team in the development and realization of their goals for the company.

The Desired Results

- To establish the current reality for the business and reach agreement on the strategic aims for the business.

- To develop in Matthew an ability to balance his preference for long-term strategic thinking with the business imperative for operational control.

- To harness the talent of his senior team so that they could help him in forming and achieving his corporate goals.

The Developing Approach

Many executives believe that having a vigorous, articulate and well-communicated picture of the goals for the business is sufficient in itself. Employees have enough common sense to test any vision against reality, and will respect senior managers who can both articulate their visions and acknowledge the current state of the business in question, i.e. what is working and not working. Conversely, working for managers where the only focus is on current issues and problems is not motivating for employees. Personal development guru Robert Fritz believes that creating anything (from a piece of music to a corporate strategy) requires the articulation of the vision, clarity on current reality and the resolution of the tension between the two. 'This tension needs resolution. The tension is a wonderful force because, as it moves toward resolution, it generates energy that is useful in creating ... Part of your job as a creator is to form this tension.'[2]

Resolving the inherent tension between the CEO's vision and his company's current position is a core skill of leadership – and one that takes time to develop and strengthen. Helping Matthew meet short-term profit objectives and position the company for the next three to five years was based on this premise. The next quarterly board meeting at which Matthew would review the company's current fiscal year and outline the proposed strategic direction for the company helped focus our minds on this objective. The aim of our first three coaching sessions was to help Matthew prepare for this board meeting.

At our first session, my goal was to ensure that Matthew had a firm and clear grasp on the company's financial and organizational situation. In advance of the meeting, Matthew had developed a first cut of a status report for the board on what had been achieved versus objectives for the current fiscal year. We focused on the main issues facing the business, the prognosis for meeting the current fiscal year's financial objectives and some key organizational concerns about the senior team. We went through this with some rigour because it was important that the board was reassured of Matthew's judgement and views after a tough previous year. I wanted to be sure that Matthew was giving a balanced and reasoned view of 'current reality' by:

● Highlighting any potential trouble spots early and not masking them from the board.

● Double-checking the logic for his and senior management's view that the company would meet its financial year projections.

● Recognizing the achievements versus the objectives for the year.

When confidence between the board and senior management has been shaken, the crucial first step is to reach agreement on the current state of the business. It is then much easier to reach agreement on the future goals when 'you are all singing from the same song sheet'.

Between our first and second sessions, Matthew met several times with his senior team to review the draft status report on the business and the financial estimates. With this in hand, we both felt confident that the senior team had a thorough and reasonable view of the current year. Our next two sessions, prior to the board meeting, focused on scoping out the strategic options for the company.

My approach, in developing the strategic options, was to first get a handle on the overall objective for growing the business. In this case, Matthew had a clear rationale for increasing shareholder value by 25–30% over the three following years. Our next step was to flesh out how this could happen. We approached this by articulating three key questions that needed to be answered.

1. Would the prospective synergies between the two business streams be sufficient to deliver 30% growth in shareholder value?

2. Could the two business streams, managed by a holding company but run as separate entities, deliver the 30%?

3. Would shareholders be better off if all or part of the businesses were sold or merged with a competitor?

We then sketched out preliminary hypotheses for these questions and a list of tasks, next steps, and analyses necessary to answer them. Between the second and third sessions, Matthew, his senior team and investment bankers (who had already started to explore question 3) set about addressing these issues. I was not present for these meetings but was privy to their final analysis and recommendations. It had emerged that other firms were interested in buying parts of the business and so there was an added sense of urgency to answering these questions.

For our third meeting, Matthew prepared a very preliminary draft of the strategic options for the business. It proposed to increase shareholder value through:

- Focusing the two businesses on targeted client sectors. (There was sufficient experience and success on several projects to demonstrate that the operating and investing skills of the business provided a unique and competitive offering.)

- Operating in three current key regions with limited piloting of the company's business model in two new regions.

- Re-organizing the businesses and the Corporate Centre to make this happen. (Considerable change in structures, some senior management attitudes and supporting reward structures would need to be part of the re-organization.)

In the end, selling all or part of the two core businesses did not make sense given the state of world markets and the values placed on this business' sector. However, continued disposal of some non-performing businesses was still sensible.

Matthew wanted to use our session to test the logic and play devil's advocate on their approach and implementation initiatives, as part of his preparation for the upcoming board meeting. I split the session into two parts: an external and internal perspective. The first part, on the external perspective, was aimed at ensuring that Matthew and his team had done an in-depth analysis of the company's competitive advantages and disadvantages in its two main business streams. In particular, was the strategy of offering operating and investing capability to clients sufficiently compelling and different versus other companies'? The analysis said 'a qualified yes' because they were first in the market with the idea but competitors were catching up. The company would need to move quickly and successfully to maintain its competitive edge.

This led to the second part of our session, which focused on what needed to happen to achieve the strategic aims in the next three years, i.e. the gap between current reality and the goals for the business. Matthew and his team had already scoped out the core implementation objectives. We devoted our time to ensuring that the initiatives were logical and complete, and to giving Matthew some time to reflect out loud some of his concerns about the implementation – mostly centred on the ability of some senior management to push through the changes. The broad initiatives were to:

- Reduce overhead costs.

- Re-organize some elements of the two business streams and the Corporate Centre to enable a global service to clients.

- Strengthen some of the functional skills of the businesses.

- Delay major ventures in new countries for the time being.

In closing the session, we agreed that Matthew would structure the next draft of his board presentation to answer three key questions:

1. Where is the business now (current reality)? – this would be a realistic health check on the companies progress in the current fiscal year.

2. What strategy will support a 30% growth in shareholder value over the next three years (vision for the business)?

3. What are the core initiatives that will get the company to this goal?

We agreed that I would comment on the draft via e-mail and telephone over the next week.

The board concurred with most, but not all, of Matthew's assessment of the company's progress and approved the overall plan for the next three years. They reinforced the view that the senior management needed to focus on operational improvements, in particular a $100 million reduction in overheads and operating costs, over the next several months and should steer away from pursuing acquisitions until the cost reduction was well on its way. Reducing costs by over $100 million was an important next step in bridging the tension between what the company wanted to achieve and the reality of where it was.

The effective leader avoids involving themself in everything. He/she focuses on issues that are both: (1) important to the organization and *also* (2) where particular value can be added (top right-hand box)

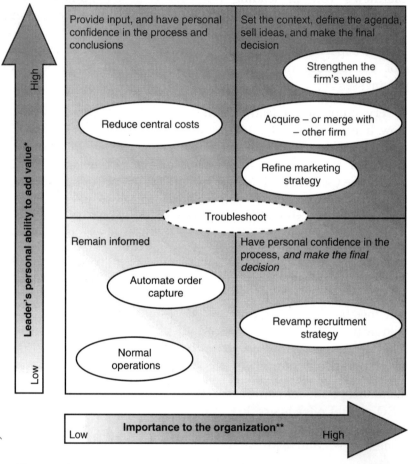

Illustrative examples (for CEO)

*Criteria: unique perspective, signalling role as figurehead, personal skills, driver of objectives for high performance, relative skills of other managers
**Criteria: impact of external reputation, impact on culture, impact on institutional skills, impact on bottom line

Figure 1.1 *Deciding how involved to become. (Source:* The Tools of Leadership, *Max Landsberg, 2000.)*

Knowing when to be 'Hands-Off' or 'Hands-On'

The focus of our coaching after the board meeting shifted to Matthew's role in leading the cost-reduction initiative. Most managers at any level in an organization need to face the dilemma of how involved they should become in issues, projects, task forces, departments, etc. This is intensified for CEOs, who must not get pulled into micro-managing individuals, projects or businesses.

A very simple and effective framework to help CEOs think about how 'hands-on' they should be is the matrix outlined in Figure 1.1.[3] This framework enables them to assess the delegation style appropriate for an individual, team or initiative, and helps to define the role of the CEO. The 'ah-*ha*' for the CEO is that he or she sees how to tailor the approach to each situation. They can then determine how deeply they should get involved in an initiative or task.

In Matthew's case, re-shaping the cost base of the corporation, including the Corporate Centre, was key. The board had agreed that by reducing costs by over $100 million, and delaying some expenditure, they could deliver their short-term financial targets. They put together a steering group of Matthew's senior team and two middle management task forces – one for each of the core businesses. The steering group would guide the task forces, look at areas of overlap in the recommendations and take the final decisions.

Landsberg's model shows that, when reducing central costs, the CEO should offer his or her input and thenceforth take a hands-off approach, trusting that the process will produce the right conclusions. But Matthew had a dilemma. Taking on the chairmanship of the steering group on cost cutting would signal both the importance of the project, and a shift in his management from a strategic focus to an operational approach. However, the practicalities of his schedule meant that he would have a tough time giving this role the attention it would need.

The framework helped Matthew and I to resolve his dilemma. The task forces had the necessary skills to fulfil the mandate, in fact their members knew more about the detailed cost structures than did Matthew. They understood the businesses well, had deep financial knowledge and were given the help of outside consultants. Matthew therefore believed that a hands-off approach would be appropriate. He would attend some key meetings to make sure the task forces were on track, provide context for their efforts, and stress the importance of the project to the health of the company.

Cost cutting is always painful, and beset by objections, counter-arguments, strong emotions, and vested interests. It was paramount that Matthew should be seen by the entire organization to back the process with resolve, overall direction and commitment. He adopted the role in the lower right-hand box of the matrix – 'have personal confidence in the process, and make the final decision'.

The work of the task forces quickly highlighted the need to redefine the cost base of the Corporate Centre, which consisted of functional departments: human resources, finance, corporate development, communications (internal and external) and legal. A small project team from the Centre was set up to determine its purpose and shape. Only Matthew and the senior project team had a detailed understanding of the Corporate Centre's operations, including those that might be devolved to the new business units. Therefore, their input into the shaping of the Corporate Centre's cost base was essential, and it was crucial that Matthew should adopt the more 'hands-on' approach in the upper-right-hand box of the matrix.

Thinking deliberately about the importance of a project to the organization and the skills of the senior direct reports allowed Matthew to focus on the right issues and strike the right balance in his style. More importantly, it freed up time to focus on the necessary strategic direction of the business.

The Role of Senior Management Group

Having developed the vision in consultation with the executive board, Matthew now needed to turn that group into a team that would implement it. Matthew had surrounded himself with strong and talented executives. Over the five years of his tenure as CEO, he had tended to work on a one-to-one basis with each of his direct reports and call meetings of sub-sets of the senior team on specific issues. Meetings of the full senior group were rare, partly because of the multiregional nature of the organization. This style had worked well in the past but now the company's reach and complexity made it more difficult to co-ordinate its different parts.

Following on from the re-organization of its two core businesses, Matthew reduced the number of direct reports from 10 to five and changed some of their responsibilities to get a better balance of skills. Matthew was not making the most of their skills and input. Over the ensuing months, we spent a part of each coaching session reviewing how he could leverage the senior group more effectively.

Gaining feedback

The first step was to understand how Matthew's direct reports and Chairman perceived his leadership. I interviewed each of his direct reports and the Chairman for insights and feedback on his leadership. This is called 360-degree feedback and is a common approach in many companies. Most companies run a 360-degree process for their managers on a paper or electronic basis on a set of agreed leadership and management competencies. At board level, I prefer to conduct personal one-to-one interviews with the senior leader's reports and boss rather than rely on a paper or electronic process because:

● You are able to capture more precisely the subtleties and nuances of leadership at board level.

● A personal interview gives respondents more time to reflect on their views and expand on impressions and reactions which are most useful in providing specific and actionable feedback.

● The interviews enhance the opportunity to capture the unknown or surprise aspects of a CEO's leadership, which a paper-based exercise can miss. This is particularly true when one is trying to gauge the impact of a leader's actions, initiatives, speeches, etc.

In Matthew's case, the interviews confirmed that he had the confidence of his direct reports and Chairman. That confidence would be enhanced if he involved his senior team more fully in the strategic planning process going forward. Matthew's skill as a strategic thinker and innovator was often ahead of his colleagues' and he needed to spend more time bringing them along to gain their buy-in and commitment. Secondly, the direct reports wanted to meet more often with the full team so that they could get to know each other and the respective core businesses better. It emerged that trust and communication between two of his direct reports were poor. I sensed a risk, from this feedback, that the leadership team could become, at best, a collection of talented and strong executives, often working at cross-purposes.

In my experience, this feedback is not unusual for senior leaders in business. A lack of trust and commitment to the strategic aims of the business follows if a senior group is not involved in setting the direction for itself and the organization. Furthermore, the team runs the risk of becoming dysfunctional. The following quotation reflects my view on the key ingredient for effective senior teams.

> *The most effective teams, focusing initially on working together, get early results in their efforts to deal with important business issues and then reflect together on the manner in which they did so, thus discovering how to function as a team.*[4]

Building a More Effective Senior Team

Using the first principle that effective teams work together by tackling core business issues, Matthew set up a two-day strategy session for the senior team. We spent one of our coaching sessions developing the agenda for the session (based on input from his senior team), and discussing how he could lead the session. Matthew was anxious that the session should both address the key issues facing the business and allow for some very creative thinking on addressing these issues. The approach developed in this coaching session was to shape the two days around core issues facing the business, as opposed to having a function- or subject-driven focus (e.g. HR, Finance, etc.).

As Matthew had devised some creative and unusual approaches to the issues, we built his ideas into the agenda, as ways to stimulate thinking and let the team know the boundaries of the discussion on each issue could be quite broad. After our coaching session, Matthew sent out the proposed agenda for feedback and adapted it based on the responses from the senior group.

I did not attend the two-day session, however, informal feedback from Matthew and some of his direct reports was positive because they had all been involved in the problem solving, and Matthew had included them in the early phases of his thinking on solving some of the pressing issues.

Four weeks after the two-day strategy session, the senior team met for a full-day session. I encouraged Matthew to include in the agenda a short discussion on how well they were or were not working together. As with many senior teams, this team was very task focused and had not paid much attention to how they could work together more effectively. I suggested two simple questions to start the reflective process: 'what are we doing that makes us an effective senior group?' and 'what are we doing that gets in the way?'. Matthew was nervous about asking the questions (being a task-focused strategic person), but I pointed out to him that the two-day strategy session had been a positive experience and this would be an opportunity to reflect on this experience and build on it. I was clear with Matthew that my aim was to help the team step back and reflect on process while 'doing work together'. I believe that teams that 'problem solve *and* reflect on their processes' build on their learning and create a stronger environment that encourages honest debate, discussion and open agendas.

With some hesitancy, Matthew agreed to pose the questions, with the caveat that he would not do so if he felt too uncomfortable or it was not appropriate. At our next coaching session, Matthew was very proud that he asked the questions and even more encouraged by the responses. There was some bantering and teasing about the questions but on the whole his direct reports found the discussion useful. What worked for the team was:

- Meeting in person once a month.

- Agreeing on decisions and issues that needed the full team's input.

- Reaching agreement on the annual goals for the business.

Less effective were lack of clarity on what each team member wanted to achieve personally and professionally within the business, Matthew's tendency to move quickly on his latest ideas on strategic direction without consulting the full team, and being in multi-regional sites.

Matthew addressed the lack of clarity on personal and professional goals for his senior team and began to use technology more effectively to help overcome the multi-regional issue. He was more aware of his tendency to move too quickly on his ideas and recognized that he needed to consult with his senior team more often.

No CEO can work alone. Enrolling the senior team in developing and implementing the short- and long-term goals is critical to the success of both the CEO and the organization. Most CEOs devote considerable time and thought to the structure, skill set and rewards for their direct reports. Few CEOs reflect and act on how the senior team can work together effectively. Matthew learned the skill of doing so by understanding what he needed to do (feedback), agreeing on the common goals for the business, doing work together and beginning to reflect on how they work together.

Reaching a Resolution

If you are struggling to focus between vision and reality, ask and resolve the following questions:

- Am I spending appropriately balanced amounts of time and energy on both the short and long term?
- Do you and your team agree on the current reality?
- Am I spending my time on the right initiatives and areas?
- Are we focused on solving the right business issues?
- Am I leading my senior team effectively?
- Could we work together more effectively?
- Does my leadership style fit my organization's needs and culture?
- If not, how can a compromise between the two be reached?

I don't think re-organization is something we should be discussing right now.

Chapter 2

Getting The Organizational Structure Right

John Coleman

Context

The search for the 'Ultimate Organization' is like the search for the Holy Grail. It has interest, great promise and is, to most people, 'a good thing' – a virtuous mission. Unfortunately, just like that ancient quest, it is also demanding, time consuming and difficult and, regrettably, is no more productive. No one has found the Grail. No one has been likely to do so either, but that has never stopped anyone from making its discovery a lifetime's pursuit. So it sometimes seems to be with the intricacies of organizations.

While searching for the 'best' organizational structure, it is often forgotten that all such structures are temporary. Not many will have a life of more than a few years without requiring further change. Many require drastic surgery after much less than that. Each is in any case no more than an artefact for getting things done. No organizational structure should be an end in itself – it cannot be. Far too often, organizational change is introduced to tackle the symptoms of a problem rather than the real 'disease'. The symptoms of dysfunction in an organization are easily misinterpreted, and that can lead to a quite inappropriate diagnosis, leading to the pursuit of organizational change. It is seductive because it seems the obvious thing to do, usually because (to quote one recent client of mine) 'the existing organization just isn't working'. Hasty change introduced in such circumstances may well result in the altered structure failing to bring the hoped for improvements. Indeed it may come to be seen, in retrospect, as having added to the problems rather than diminishing them.

There are real risks in making structural changes that do not meet a clear and obvious need – or which cannot be met by an alternative solution. Yet when I look around, structural changes in organizations seem to be high on the list of remedies of first resort. One of the attractions, of course, is that a change in organizational structure can appear simple to carry through. It can be conceived within the safety of the office, need not entail much research or discussion ahead of action, and can be implemented at the drop of the proverbial hat. It is something which can be done as an imposition of will on an organization. It is an 'immediate' action, that can be performed swiftly, and one that shows very clearly 'who's the boss'. Perhaps for that reason it can be a seductive notion for anyone wanting action, movement, a visible signal of change – or who just wants to provide incontrovertible evidence that 'things are happening'. It puts a personal mark on the structure. Given the inherent dangers that lurk within most such changes, though, wholesale re-organization ought to be a rare event. It should be one to which leaders resort only after very careful weighing of the pros and cons, and the available alternatives – and an equally careful diagnosis and definition of just what problems the leader is trying to resolve. This is perhaps easier said than done, which may explain why it is done so infrequently. Too many organizations appear in a state of constant flux. There are an awful lot of 'serial re-organizers' lurking in the upper reaches of business and commerce.

There is little point in making organizational changes that have little chance of taking root, of becoming permanent. Organizations that win do so because they take great pains to ensure that, where they change, the change processes are all-embracing. This means that, above all, they address the key needs of creating strong leadership and high motivation. Contrary to popular belief, perhaps, such things rarely happen by chance. Even more rarely do they happen because of the messianic power of the appointed leader of the business. They happen because someone takes the time and trouble to think his or her way right through what is required, top to bottom, and then takes even greater pains in the communication and implementation phases. Successful re-organization is about much more than getting the right structure in place.

Where the lines are drawn on paper makes little difference if the underpinnings are not well engineered and in place. Everyone knows that we can all resent change when it happens – especially if it is imposed on us without what we see as good reason. Tinkering with organizational structures usually wastes time, energy, and resource, and squanders scarce opportunity – and it thus stands a good chance of lowering levels of motivation, not raising them. Too often, it takes so much energy and resource to get the new organization 'up and flying' that, when the dust has settled, performance is actually found to have worsened. Yet too many aspiring leaders still get the cart before the horse in this difficult and subtle area.

It also seems to be a fact that organizational structures, no matter how cleverly constructed, have quite a short shelf-life. Even when there are major obstacles to success within an organization, whether from inherent and fatal structural defects (quite rare!) or basic human shortcomings (much more common!) motivated people find ways to get business done. They become adept at working round the roadblocks, which is why it is often so instructive to map out how an organization actually works, by defining communications and information flows, as opposed to how it is meant to operate in theory. People can, and do, work well in the most arcane – or even downright bizarre – structures, provided they are clear about what they were to achieve, and provided, above all, that they are motivated to achieve it.

I have been a coach since the mid-1990s. My clients are senior leaders from a wide range of size of organizations, some large (e.g. FTSE-100 companies), some small (e.g. entrepreneurial, small companies) and many in between. The organizations themselves operate in industry, commerce, retail, the financial sector, the public sector and others.

Many of my clients – individual leaders in all sorts of organizations – come to me with the need to wrestle with organizational issues. Indeed, I am always surprised if the topic does not surface earlier rather than later. Often, it is seen as an issue that requires priority attention. As we settle down to probe the matter, I find that everyone asks: 'What sort of organizational structure is the best for me and my organization?' The more thoughtful also ask themselves: 'Should I re-organize?' This latter question often does not get the attention it deserves, as alternatives can be hard to define, and may be much more daunting a prospect than changing the organization. The big surprise is that so few people start off with the more fundamental issue of: 'What, *precisely,* are the difficulties or issues I wish to resolve here?' As a result, only a part of their problems – usually the most obvious part – gets resolved. The organizational shape is changed, but too often the underlying issues are not tackled. To help to explore this further, let us look at a fairly typical client.

Client Company Profile

Within Leisure Co, there are three 'divisions' of broadly equal size – High Street Retail, Travel, and Air. Air, which retails in airports, is a relatively recent acquisition. There is also a small (approximately £10 million per annum turnover) 'New Markets' division that pioneers and develops new service offers before handing them on to the three other businesses. This division had grown in four years from small project beginnings, but where it should fit in the organization has been the subject of recent debate.

Leisure Co had a turnover of roughly £185 million, annual profits of about £13 million. It needs to spend in the order of £5 million a year for the next four years to upgrade its existing operations and premises. It is headquartered to the west of London and, while it operates mainly in the UK, has about a one-fifth of its business in Europe – where there seems to be great potential for expansion. It has a little over 2600 direct employees, but within that number makes use of varying (but not inconsiderable) numbers of part-time employees.

Client Profile

Dermot is 38, a New Zealander. He arrived in the UK with an honours degree in modern languages, and joined a media company in Birmingham. He worked there for three years, learning the basics of selling and marketing, before moving on to spend two years in London. Next came a US secondment, based first in Philadelphia, and subsequently in Miami, in a senior marketing role for Latin America. He married his Australian wife during his four years in the United States.

Seven years ago he left his company, taking six months out to return to Wellington, and spending time in Melbourne before returning to the UK. After a spell job hunting, Dermot joined Leisure Co, and soon moved up into general management. He is a 'rising star', and when we met had already built a solid reputation, and was expected to make the board of Leisure Co sooner rather than later.

The Challenge

Dermot ran a Leisure Co business stream, operating within an intensely competitive market place in which his business was seen as an important player, but not a dominant one. Its track record over the past five years had been somewhat mixed, with progress on expanding its market share in a growing retail market, and reasonable revenue growth, but with a declining level of profitability.

The parent company believed that there were significant growth opportunities away from the business's traditional markets. While it would fund judicious acquisitions, it wished Dermot's business stream to fund its own rapid organic growth in addition. Thus there was pressure on Dermot, who had assumed the leadership of his business six months previously, for an immediate and sustained improvement in profitability, and a prompt acceleration of the rates of growth. He had considerable freedom to produce the required results, but needed help in using that freedom in a disciplined way.

The challenge became clear. It was to push Dermot to ensure that his diagnosis of the problem was a good one – to make sure that he did not regard the change of organization he was proposing as the end of the change process. To help in this, I would explore with him some alternative views which might just lead to him discovering a more fitting solution to his business' larger – although underlying – issues. A secondary challenge was to help Dermot find effective ways of communicating what he was about – to all of his business's stakeholders, and not least to his boss, who was looking for a quick fix from Dermot.

The Desired Results

● To conduct a more probing diagnosis of Leisure Co's performance problems.

● To identify and think through a more comprehensive way forward for my client, which made the most of what he had to offer.

● To help manage the expectations of his boss effectively.

The Developing Approach

Dermot and I had met only twice when the subject of re-organization came up. He told me this was something he had to do at once, and that Frank – his boss and CEO of the parent company, Procellaris – was keen for him to get on with it. According to Dermot, once he had 'sorted out' the organizational structure, he would invest the majority of his own time, energies and abilities in driving the business forward much harder and faster. He would then see how his team performed, and perhaps seek some replacements if, by year-end, things were not getting back on target.

I pricked up my ears, knowing it was barely 18 months since Frank had insisted on the last big corporate re-organization. I had been told Dermot's own business had been through some sort of organizational upheaval every two years or so for the past five years, and also knew that Leisure Co's performance had remained stubbornly flat. The last re-organization had failed to achieve any quick lift in performance, and had apparently reduced morale to an all-time low.

Dermot's approach seemed to be driven more by the need for rapid action, and his high self-confidence, than by sound strategy. I needed to persuade him to accept the challenge of attempting a more thoughtful diagnosis of the problems facing him, which we could talk through in order to lead him to a solution that had a greater chance of success. His business needed more than a quick change of organization and a new burst of energy.

I began by inviting Dermot to tell me more about his present organization. He sketched it out:

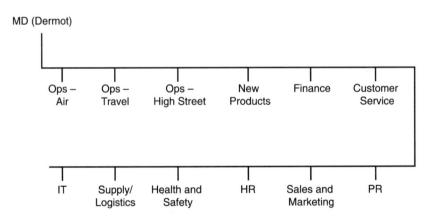

MD (Dermot)

| Ops – Air | Ops – Travel | Ops – High Street | New Products | Finance | Customer Service |

| IT | Supply/ Logistics | Health and Safety | HR | Sales and Marketing | PR |

All twelve of these 'Directors' reported to Dermot. This was a historic legacy – and a complete nonsense. Also, he was clear that he should reconsider his functional resources, as a matter of urgency. He saw that as having implications not just for Leisure Co, but also for the parent group. He was clear about Finance, HR, and Sales and Marketing, none of which presented insuperable issues.

Finance, for example, was run by a Director who, as well as being Leisure Co's Finance Director, was the corporate Deputy

Controller. In that role, Jane ran the 'people development' and succession planning systems for the Procellaris group's Finance function. Dermot believed it important that he had a Leisure Co Finance chief dedicated fully to his business. Jane was ambitious, though, and would not lightly give up her corporate activities, which she felt positioned her well within the Finance function. She was a strong performer, and Dermot wanted to keep her in Leisure Co – but in a role with less ambiguity. He recognized it would not be easy to persuade her.

He had no problems in HR. He respected Colin, who had headed up the function in Leisure Co for years, and used Colin as a sounding board for his own thinking about organizational changes. While he admitted Colin was not a particularly strategic thinker, there was no doubt where his loyalties lay.

In Sales and Marketing, he had a different problem. There was a dedicated Leisure Co Director, but the issue was whether James was up to scratch. Although popular and energetic, he had won his spurs by performing strongly in Sales. He had little Marketing background, and understood selling much better. Dermot, an ex-marketeer, was frustrated by insufficient analysis of markets, key customers and potential growth areas. Marketing was not giving a strong lead. As a consequence, Dermot was considering a split, leaving Sales teams reporting to the leaders of the business streams (High St., Travel, etc.) and importing a new Marketing Director. It would leave James without a job.

He was less clear about IT, Customer Service, Supply/Logistics, PR, and Health & Safety. He saw scope in the 'surrender' of some elements of functional management to the corporate (i.e. Procellaris) central functions. This should give him much-needed cost-cutting opportunities, and he believed the powerful central functions should add greater value to his business than at present. He recognized that he would have to negotiate the details of these aspects of his new organization with the Procellaris central function heads, but had no anxieties on that score. What he proposed looked as follows:

MD (Dermot)

Dir –	Dir –	Dir –	Finance Dir	HR Dir
High Street	Air and Travel	Marketing and		
		New Products		

This combined the previously separate Air and Travel businesses, which had some generic similarities. It also combined responsibility for New Products – always something of a hybrid as a business in Leisure Co – with the accountability for Marketing. Sales teams, and all other functional teams, would be run in the business units by the Business Directors, but would have strong 'dotted lines' to the respective Leisure Co directors in Finance and HR. The rest of the functions would have rather weaker 'dotted lines' to the relevant Procellaris functional heads. As far as it went this was sensible, and in the long run would probably help sharpen the way Leisure Co was managed. In the immediate future, though, it would not solve all the issues for Dermot.

I had developed several concerns of my own about those issues. An over-arching one emerged early and I kept bringing us back to it. This was the matter of what hard facts Dermot had to support his belief that organization change would deliver what was needed in Leisure Co. He had already admitted, a bit defensively, 'Well, a lot of it's gut instinct'. I was convinced that he needed a re-think before charging into action. Since I was sure he was wrong, I needed to understand his thinking. I wanted to be sure he was totally clear about what he wished the new organization to achieve, and about what caused the present structure to under-perform. As we discussed this, even Dermot admitted he was beginning to find himself less than convincing about why the new structure would be a sure-fire success where the old one (and its predecessors) had failed. I saw this as progress.

My second concern was even more fundamental, and centred on how the business' customers and suppliers would perceive yet another re-organization. There were as yet no answers to this, but

Dermot, nobody's fool, was well aware that his business had wrestled for years, through several re-organizations, with similar problems to those he now faced. While he found my probing and challenging irritating, he was coming round to the idea that he might need a more all-embracing strategy if he was to build good foundations for his success as an MD. These needed to take in a wider range of issues than that of how many people Dermot had responding to him. We agreed to focus on these.

Dermot had a lot at stake and could not afford to produce a real 'turkey' at this point in his career. The starting situation looked like this:

- Time was pressing.

- He was no longer 'new' in his role.

- His remit was to make rapid progress in sorting out the business, which was still not performing

- I thought that performance would not be much altered by re-drawing the organizational lines – Dermot was not convinced, but couldn't demonstrate the contrary.

- I felt that his hope that a new structure combined with even harder driving from him would improve performance was a huge gamble for the business, and for Dermot personally.

- He and his team were already working flat out, and we had even discussed at our first meeting whether the pace was sustainable in the long run. An organizational re-shuffle would add greatly to that load, not just in the short term.

- Everyone would have to learn how the new structure and relationships would actually work. This would take time, which Dermot didn't have. Also, it was a good bet that the 'new ways' would not be exactly as Dermot anticipated, or wished.

Looking back over Leisure Co's recent history, it was clear that much wasted time and energy had gone into each preceding organizational change. On each occasion, there had been a period of confusion – chaos, almost – followed by a longish period of adjust-ment. The changes created extra stresses and absorbed huge effort which should have been put into pursuing more direct ways of raising bottom-line performance. Repeatedly 're-shuffling the pack' became damaging and sapped confidence.

Dermot shared most of these concerns, and had lately heard that, among 'the troops', there was an impression that the top of the organization, i.e. Dermot, was flailing around. The constant organizational changes had begun to look like ineffective leadership. That was dangerous territory. Dermot bridled when I suggested that the serial re-organizations had been manifestations of weak management, lacking the 'heart' to create and communicate a strong vision of the necessary performance level, as well as the tenacity to pursue its vision ruthlessly with an existing management structure.

Setting that aside and looking forward, though, it would obviously be better to use all available energy to pursue performance targets directly, rather than risk dissipating it in yet another re-organization. This was not to rule out organizational change. It was more to make it a consequence of other strategies, not a strategy in its own right.

Both of us concurred that true success came from delivering extraordinary results from ordinary organizations. From there we worked round to the proposition that the vision, quality, visibility and motivational skills of the leaders were of far greater importance than where lines were drawn on paper. Accepting that, the ques-tion began to focus on how to be a more effective leader. That had little direct connection with structuring the next organizational changes, even though changes were needed.

Other issues surfaced as we talked. People in different parts of Leisure Co tenaciously preserved their own sub-cultures, especially where their original culture had been strong and self-sustaining. As a consequence the culture – 'the way we do things round here' – in Dermot's businesses was far from uniform. This might not matter where the former entity remained as a discrete sub-group, but if a new structure were put in place that mixed two different and hitherto separate working cultures, friction could follow. What Dermot was initially considering in putting together the Air and Travel businesses took little account of this and there were no plans for it to be tackled. Ploughing ahead on the intended basis thus threatened to produce more heat than light in at least one segment of the business.

At our next session, Dermot admitted to another concern. This was the matter of whether Leisure Co – or indeed Procellaris – had the right calibre of senior staff to populate a new organizational structure to his satisfaction. He had become aware that there were 'quite a few tired, over-promoted people in big jobs', and was not confident that they could perform in the present structure or a successor organization. He also worried that Frank, who knew some of these people from way back, would not permit him to make a clean sweep. In any event, he suspected Frank was planning some re-structuring in the parent's European operations, so there would be fierce competition for the best available people. Thus there was no guarantee that Dermot would get the sort of performers he needed, and any new structure would inevitably start off with many of the present middle and senior management, even though many roles would be different.

We reflected that there was not a lot of glory to be gained from setting up a new structure which kept all the old lags. New blood would be needed, but first a fierce determination to 'Change the people – or change the people' might generate more constructive ways forward than re-drawing organizational lines. In other words, trying to change the motivations and mind-sets of key people should be the starting point – though the option of changing (removing) those who failed to respond must remain an option.

There was a lot to ponder. Dermot had relinquished the notion of a change in organization being an answer, in itself, to his performance problems. He still believed that changes in the structure were needed, but now saw that there were bigger issues that must be addressed at the same time. Above all, to my relief, he had convinced himself that the obvious problems had to be tackled *now*, not set aside for consideration after embarking on a new organization, and that in doing so he would not be taking the easy option.

Meanwhile, there was no mistaking Frank's push for 'drastic action'. It had become a daily topic of conversation. Frank sought clear evidence of change, so would see launching a wholesale re-structuring as Dermot taking dynamic action to impose himself on the business. He might not be easy to convince that there was a stronger alternative, particularly since it would take great effort to plan, communicate, implement and drive. It would also be likely to muddy the waters for maybe a year, we estimated, while new people found their feet, and new ways of behaving kicked in. It would have huge upsides, and would be less of a gamble in performance terms though, ironically, a 'quick and dirty' re-organization would be less of a gamble politically.

Set against that, Dermot could reduce the risks of failure by tackling head-on the issues he could identify as limiting performance. The biggest danger was that in the early stages he might appear to Frank, and thus to the board, as insufficiently vigorous or bold. This worried Dermot, and rightly. If that perception took root, he would be moved on without compunction. We worked at this by looking at the four issues we had identified as those the original re-organization had been meant to resolve.

First, Dermot needed to set out his vision for the new Leisure Co. This needed to be bold – certainly more than meeting the budgetary targets, difficult though that might be. He already had a clear idea of the shape and size of business he wanted to create. He was also working on the customer and market facing aspects, but had so far not given much thought to the business culture. He admitted the present culture was lacklustre, and found it difficult to single out anything really special or emotive about it. Yet, if his organization were to be a top performer, it needed to attain the extra 'something special' all outstanding teams possess. It was ultimately up to him to create and sustain this.

Dermot raised the question of what ought to be the guiding values of the business. As he observed, 'good businesses always seem to have great people – and clear values'. He would add values into his vision, he decided. I cautioned him against getting too airy-fairy, and urged him to focus on stipulating the required behaviours, since these would be easier to define, target and track. The advantages of working to change behaviours were self-evident. The organization was already too big to be driven by the will of a single individual, so the issue of motivation would remain to the fore. People had to be better motivated, inspired even, if the business were to meet expectations. That need for inspiration meant a significant leadership challenge for Dermot, who would need to work through a coherent business vision and then roll out its communication across the business.

Second, he had to deal with the question marks against some of the potentially key players. Dermot categorized the 20 top people into three boxes by considering skills, personality and current performance against the company's competencies, his own observations and his future intentions regarding the culture he wanted for his team. By the end of the session we had seeded 11 people in the first box ('OK – No problems'); six in the second box ('Must lift their game'); and three in the third ('Unsatisfactory'). Dermot would probably need to replace three senior people and 're-programme and renew' six others. How he set about this would help set the style of the organization. He had to do it in a way that would be seen as fair, open and 'above board', but needed to start off with the ongoing team in place. It would be a major error to begin to build a new culture with managers not destined to remain, and he should ensure his prime team was composed as he wished from the outset.

Third, Dermot needed to think through and define *exactly* what he expected people to achieve, and what their personal roles and accountabilities would be for the future. He determined that he would personally introduce this absolute clarity, starting with his direct team, by expounding on his own role as he now saw it before going on to lay out his expectations of them. He would focus primarily on behaviours as a preliminary step towards setting detailed performance targets and measures. This would require a lot of pre-work, as he would have embarked on something much more complex than the originally intended organizational re-hash. It would take longer but, once done, would underpin a huge change in the business. He also needed to consider how to communicate 'the new Leisure Co' to its customer base, and set this aside as a subsidiary but vital project for his team to tackle.

The fourth area was that of measurement. Dermot believed in the old saw that 'What don't get measured, don't get improved', so we needed to set the prime measures of success for what was beginning to look and feel like a substantial transformation programme. The question of measures was not just about the key financial, logistical measures and satisfaction-tracking measures, which were relatively straightforward. The complication was that there also had to be ways of charting progress towards the achievement of the vision at its broadest. This in turn meant finding measures for, among other things, employee and managerial morale and motivation, external customer and supplier satisfaction, general internal levels of satisfaction, performance relative to the competition and so on. 'None of that's rocket science', Dermot pronounced with his usual confidence. All the same, he agreed that it required careful thought and agreement from his entire team, followed by a careful process of 'advocacy' down through the whole organization.

On the way through the four issues, we recognized that there was, in fact, an 'umbrella' fifth – and so we turned to what might be called the political aspects. These revolved for the most part around issues of communication, on the one hand; and of managing Frank (and to a lesser extent, the board) on the other. The two were inter-linked. We already knew Frank had clear expectations of rapid action and results. According to Dermot, he was part way towards regarding a rehash of Leisure Co's organizational structure as an essential component of that, so there was a need to manage his perceptions quite carefully. This was especially true of the early stages.

Managing Frank's expectations was going to be as important as managing those of his own team, business or customers. If Dermot made a mess of this part of the process, managing the rest of the transformation could become, for him, a purely academic question. Dermot decided to involve his immediate team, some of whom had known Frank 'man and boy', in considering this issue.

Above all in this, Dermot needed to be happy that he had a way forward which was not just communicable, but also wholly acceptable to Frank and the main board. As well as being able to explain what his transformation was about, he needed cogent reasons why his way forward was better than 'instant' re-organization. He had to demonstrate that there were compelling extra business gains to be had. We rehearsed the arguments on both sides, until Dermot pronounced himself satisfied that he could convince Frank the new course was the right one, even if it was less of an 'instant cure' than might have been wished.

Communicating with the business as a whole was also a vital part of Dermot's leadership. It needed to be built around the themes and behaviours from his vision, which led us to spend time talking about 'walking the talk'. This was not just about being seen to behave in accordance with the values and strategy of the business vision, though that was of huge importance. It was also about being a role model, visibly guided by that same overall vision and strategy. There was a need to ensure others – especially the top team – behaved according to the same tenets. Many management teams fail to handle this aspect well. There should be a very low tolerance of 'out of line' behaviours, not just for the body of the organization, but for those at its head. All too often senior teams are blind to the impact of their own behaviours, which then give out powerful and mostly negative messages. This behavioural part of change was simple to talk about. The difficulty was in driving it – and that was where Dermot would need all his energy and enthusiasm in the long haul. There was no 'quick fix' in this, and dogged persistence was usually of greater value than showmanship.

'Well,' Dermot reflected in one of our last coaching sessions, 'I am certainly doing a re-organization.' He was indeed.

What he now planned was a long way from his start-point. He had begun with three aims: to sharpen accountabilities by re-drawing his organization; to replace those he thought were failing; and to drive long-term performance by increasing the pressures on managers. The latter he would have attempted by his personal efforts – by force of personality married to power of office. I speculated that, while there would have been rapid change, it would never have developed the roots to ensure permanence. In a couple of years Dermot, or perhaps his successor, would have re-organized yet again, on the back of another set of unacceptable results.

Did Dermot succeed? Well, he's still at it. He started well, and convinced Frank that his course was the right one – though it was not all sweetness and light, since Frank said in agreeing to give Dermot his head: 'On your own head be it!' Dermot so far seems to be winning, though not fast enough to keep Frank off his tail. However, there *is* a new spirit taking shape in Leisure Co, and the business trends are now in the right direction. Dermot is still finding new angles in his change plans, and believes absolutely in his ability to drive this change process to completion. I believe he will win though.

Reaching a Resolution

- What is the factual evidence and hard data – not the assumptions, acts of faith or hunches?

- Is your analysis of the situation totally honest? Have you shared your thinking with a trusted advisor?

- What is your unifying vision of the future that your people can understand, empathize with and use to inform their decision making and targeting?

- What are the behaviours expected in order to build success? Are you modelling them, championing them, insisting on them?

- Do you have the right calibre of people to drive change with you? If not, re-organization alone will *not* deliver the business.

- Have you steeled yourself to be brave? In a bad situation, bold action is required, but all too often the action taken proves to be 'too little, too late'.

Can I just have a quick word?

Chapter 3

Creating Time To Maximize CEO Impact

Elspeth May

Context

Every well-run business has a long-term strategy. It is ultimately the task of the CEO to determine that strategy, communicate it to those working in the organization and make it happen. Sounds straightforward enough, but the problem for most CEOs of public companies is that they are judged and rewarded on short-term results. All too easily, day-to-day operational issues muscle their way into the CEO's agenda and the siren voices of the media and financial analysts call for progress over much shorter time-scales than used to be the case. Not so many years ago, the CEO would be called to account once a year, facing shareholders and press at the AGM. Now, many are expected to produce weekly progress reports for those outside with an interest in the organization. So how do CEOs pull themselves out of the pressures of the day-to-day to add most value on long-term big picture issues? That is what we shall be exploring in this chapter.

Many CEOs have said that theirs is a lonely job. The CEO is the focus of everyone's attention as shown in Figure 3.1.

Faced with an ever-increasing pace of change and near-overload in terms of data, managing time becomes the main day-to-day priority of any CEO. So many people want part of that time – the board, the senior executives, other employees, shareholders, investment bankers, analysts, the media and even the CEO's family and friends!

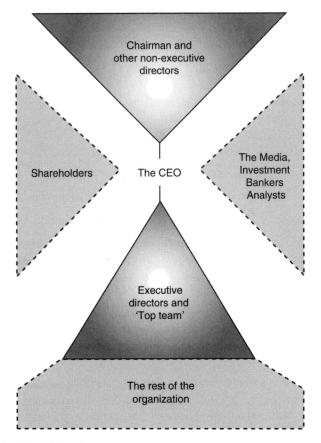

Figure 3.1 *CEO stakeholders.*

For many CEOs, getting the right home/work balance becomes a Utopia they seek, sadly, in vain.

Despite being surrounded by people, it is hard for a CEO to find anyone to confide in especially when things go wrong. With whom can they share doubts about the long-term strategy, for example? Or, discuss the competence of senior board members? Or just talk to about the huge pressures of the job? This is where a coach can be especially effective by acting as a confidante and empathic listener.

Much attention is focused on newly appointed CEOs. The pressure to make an impact – fast – is growing. It helps, in the early days of being a CEO to buy some time. The key to this is having a vision for the future of the organization and being able to articulate convincingly a longer-term strategy that will deliver this. If the financial analysts like what they hear – and they will, if they can see that the strategy is backed up by hard numbers and evidence of potential return to shareholders – the immediate pressure diminishes while they wait to see if the CEO can deliver.

But they won't wait long.

If the strategy is going to work, one of the key tasks of the CEO is to build an effective team. This is essential if the CEO is to manage the workload. Having a strong, capable top team enables the CEO to delegate much of the running of the business, including strategy formulation, to them. It also gives greater credibility to the organization, which will be seen as not reliant on the effort and ideas of just one person.

Often, building that team becomes an endless quest to which some CEOs end up devoting much of their time. Monitoring performance of the senior executives, planning for succession, and identifying new recruits for the senior team to plug any skills-gaps are tasks only the CEO can fulfil. They demand an ability to identify and nurture talent. Making these judgements and decisions about people can create a significant pressure for the CEO, especially since this is an area where there is often little internal support, except perhaps from the non-executive directors.

Feeling you are not in control of how you spend your time can create a sense of powerlessness and stress. In theory, as the people at the top, CEOs should be able to choose how they allocate their time. Some can do this, but too often do so by focusing on the activities they enjoy or being in the places which suit them. One CEO I worked with lived in the north of England and spent every Friday visiting the subsidiary closest to his home, even though its turnover represented just 5% of the group's sales. With much of the rest of his time spent in the head office in London, he only spent about a one-third of his time visiting the remaining 95% of the business, spread around the UK and Europe. He did have some control over how he spent his time, but did not use it in the most effective way for the business.

Most CEOs I have spoken to say that they would like to spend more of their time thinking and planning for the future, but there are many barriers to this. Typical things that get in the way of long-term planning include:

- too many meetings

- too great a span of control (many CEOs now have up to 15 direct reports)

- rehearsing for and debriefing after meetings

- issues related to the senior team – personality clashes, gaps in the team, high turnover in the team, etc.

- e-mails, faxes, phone messages and other interruptions.

Add to this list the probability of acquisitions, mergers, strategic alliances and other deals along the way, and there is considerable scope for the CEO to be blown off course when it comes to long-term planning. But staying focused on the need to manage time effectively is the only way in which CEOs can achieve what is necessary for their organizations and, most importantly, for themselves. This is potentially a highly stressful job for which the CEO needs a strong sense of self-belief and excellent support from family, friends and colleagues to keep the pressures at bay.

Some of the strategies I recommended to my client Alice may seem obvious – but knowing one *should* employ them does not necessarily lead to doing so! I hope that seeing them in action will help to demonstrate how easily they can be put in place – and how effective they can be.

Client Company Profile

'Girl' is a large UK public company, a high-street retailer of teen and twenties fashion. It has an international element, though the bulk of its turnover (£1+ billion) is in the UK, from stores rather than mail order or Internet. The executive and non-executive boards each have 10 directors. At this time there was no chairman in place, which added to the CEO's difficulties, as the Chair would usually be a prime source of wise counsel.

The Client

Alice had been in post for just a few months when we started our work together. She had arrived at her present position by working her way up through the company rather than being brought in from outside. Having started on the shop floor, she had progressed to an important fashion buyership, which had attracted a considerable amount of media attention. From there she had moved to the CEO position, at the age of 46, when the previous CEO retired.

Alice is married to Iain, a self-employed architect. They have had no children, but Iain has two daughters aged 18 and 20 from a previous marriage, both at university. Alice had a good relationship with her step-daughters but was becoming concerned that the demands of her job meant she saw a lot less of them than in the past.

The Challenge

The fundamental challenge was to explore how Alice could resist the temptation to mire herself in day-to-day operations. In working together, our goal was to explore in depth how she spent her time, and compare that with how she felt she *should* be spending it in order to be fully effective rather than merely surviving.

At the heart of this was a question: what can the CEO – and only the CEO – do to add value to the organization? If we could answer that, we had a starting point for moving forward and setting Alice's future focus.

I had expected it to be hard to find time in her diary for our coaching sessions, but, particularly in the absence of a Chair, Alice was determined to make time. She desperately needed someone in whom she could confide, and who would help her to organize her time for the coming months.

The Desired Results

- To gain an understanding of how Alice was spending her time.
- To re-focus time-management on the priority tasks.
- To ensure Alice was getting all the information she needed.
- To avoid information overload by assessing what was critical and what could be filtered out.
- To gain a better home/work balance.
- To develop strategies for handling stress-inducing media attention.

The Developing Approach

All CEOs work long hours. It goes with the territory. Those in retailing have the added challenge that their world truly is 24/7. So, having spent our first meeting gaining a thorough understanding of Alice's organization and her role in it, I asked Alice to keep a log of how she spent her time over a month. (This task itself takes time, but it is worth doing to understand fully where the hours go each day. An efficient personal assistant can create this log.) We then reviewed it at a subsequent meeting. A typical week for Alice looked like this:

Visiting stores	1 day
Acquiring/assimilating information	1.5 days
Planning and working with other people	2 days
Board work and dealing with external stakeholders	1 day
Operational matters	1.5 days
Total	7 days

This punishing schedule left little free time for Alice's family, friends and outside work interests. Often her week's 'social life' came down to corporate hospitality. Add to this the fact that most, if not all, of her planning work ended up being done at home, and it is easy to see why she needed a very patient and supportive partner.

While reviewing how Alice spent her time, we concluded that she faced a number of realities:

● She was the ultimate decision-maker.

● It is all too easy to let others dictate how time is spent. She needed to take control.

● To inform her strategic thinking, she needed to digest a huge volume of information: daily sales figures; competitors' results; analysts' reports; board papers – the list goes on … .

● She spent more time than she had anticipated preparing for, and debriefing after, board and other key meetings.

● It is easy to get distracted! Even when there is no acquisition or hostile takeover in the air, there are mundane distractions. E-mails probably come top of this list, so developing a system for filtering and monitoring of e-mails is essential. Here again is where an excellent personal assistant can be invaluable.

I asked Alice to think about how she could get a grip on these realities and manage the many pressures on her time. We looked at how she should be spending her time, and to do this I used a model to illustrate the types of activity in which senior executives can engage – this is shown in Figure 3.2.

It was no surprise to find that the urgent and important tasks tended to take over. Dealing with crises and tight deadlines often led to a fire-fighting style of management, with many of the deadlines and crises determined by other people. Short-term interrup-

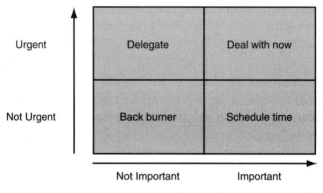

Comparing this with how she actually spent her time was an interesting exercise. All too frequently, reality looked like this:

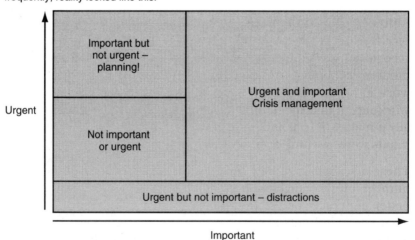

Figure 3.2 *Time management. (Adapted from* The Seven Habits of Highly Effective People *by Stephen Covey. Simon & Schuster. Copyright © Stephen R Covey, 1989.)*

tions – the phone, the fax, the e-mail, people 'popping in for a chat' – created a disjointed pattern of working with very little time for thinking and planning. Ideally, a CEO should aim to spend most of his or her time on tasks in the bottom right-hand corner of Figure 3.2 – the important but not urgent tasks. These are the tasks that take time and add most value: planning, strategic thinking, and building relationships with key stakeholders (such as major shareholders).

Having gained an insight into how her time was actually being spent, Alice and I explored how it should be spent. Alice realized, once she looked at the data from the month when her time was monitored, that she was spending too much time reacting to others' demands. She had always favoured an 'open-door' culture in Girl. She wanted anyone in the organization to feel they could talk to her. She wanted to feel approachable, but realized that she would have to control colleagues' access to her if she was to get anything done.

We discussed what steps Alice could take to re-prioritize her time. Top of the list was how to create more 'thinking time'. Alice chose to do this by booking time in her diary for fictitious meetings to create thinking space, and taking some time out of her office.

Attitudes to working from home have undergone a great shift in recent years. What was previously seen as taking things easy, is now recognized as a potentially very efficient way of working. With modern technology and communications, it is easy for a CEO to work at home occasionally and still stay in touch with the office. Working out how much time to spend away from the office is generally a matter of trial and error; Alice and I were able to review how things were working over several months.

These discussions of how time was being spent took place over a number of coaching sessions. Once I felt that Alice had a much better understanding of where time went, I asked her to consider what she – and only she – could do to help Girl. I wanted her to give serious thought to this issue so that we could discuss it at our next meeting. In thinking about this, I reminded Alice to consider the purpose of the organization? I hesitate to use the word 'mission' as it has become rather over-used, and it is often associated with platitude-laden statements for public consumption, rather than reflections on how the company will act. (Judging by actions rather than words is invariably more effective.)

Like many CEOs, Alice saw as her primary purpose creating the vision for Girl and building its top team. In Chapter 1 Heather Dawson dealt with how a CEO can get his top team to help with the creation of that vision, while in Chapter 5 Sue Godfrey discusses how to align the top team with the corporate strategy. So I have focused here on how Alice could build the right team, so that tasks could be delegated to them.

Alice and I addressed this by looking at these issues:

- What could she delegate *now* to other members of her top team? These needed to be tasks others could take on without the need for any training or support.

- What could she delegate to others if she provided some initial coaching and support? For example, her Finance Director was already doing an excellent job of taking the strategic plan and working it up into figures, but he did not yet feel comfortable communicating that financial strategy to financial institutions and the media. Alice decided to arrange for him to have some specific media training and then worked with him to enhance the part he played in the external communication process.

- What can't she give away? We were back with the issue of what only she could do!

I asked Alice to describe how she planned her time, wondering to what extent she delegated this part of her work. It emerged that she left it almost entirely to her PA, who was more disciplined about booking thinking time, for example, than Alice was. This worked well, because her PA had a very clear understanding of Alice's priorities, but I reminded Alice that, ultimately, she must decide for herself how to spend her time.

To help her with this, we addressed the following questions:

- How do you manage your time, e.g. to-do lists, time planners, use of PA?

- What works well with this system?

- What does not work well?

- What three things could you do to align more closely how you spend your time with how you should spend your time?

This is about reviewing the *process* of time management. One of the techniques I suggested Alice might like to try was taken from W. Timothy Gallwey's book *The Inner Game of Work*.[2] This was to tell herself to 'STOP!' before undertaking an activity, and give herself the opportunity to think through whether she should be doing it in the first place. She took up Gallwey's suggestion of creating a 'STOP!' sign in her office to remind her of the importance of asking herself: 'Is this activity a priority?', i.e. an important but not urgent task? Is it so urgent that it *must* be done now? Should I be doing this or can someone else do it? If I do this now, what other activity will it supersede? (A CEO is never just waiting around for something to do!) This process only takes up a few seconds, and is a very simple way of keeping focused on how time should be spent.

Having created space for thinking time, we explored what information Alice was receiving, and how well, or badly, it matched up with her needs. In most large organizations, information flows are well established and the focus is on key performance indicators appropriate to the business. But sometimes, reports continue to be produced because 'they always have been', while the business has evolved making them redundant. So, I suggested that Alice should carry out a systematic review of what information she was receiving and ask herself the following questions:

- Do I need this information?

- Could someone else make better use of it?

- Do I need all this information or merely a summary?

- Am I receiving it on a sufficiently timely basis, and at the right intervals?

- What would happen if I did not receive this information?

- Could I receive it in a different form, e.g. e-mail, fax, phone call, intranet, etc?

This review led to a reduction in the reported information Alice needed to receive.

My job as a coach is to ask questions in a way that enables clients to think in different ways, to see problems from different perspectives and to consider possibilities they may have overlooked. One of the questions that served this purpose well was asking Alice: 'How do you know people are telling you the truth, not just telling you what they want you to hear?' Of course, this is a question that is relevant to everyone who has to rely on information from other colleagues, but given the pivotal position of the CEO it is especially important that he or she get to the truth of what is going on. When we reflected on this Alice identified a number of ways in which she could 'test' information she received:

- She would use her previous experience of functional areas within the business to help her evaluate information.

- She would ask herself: 'Does it feel right?' Often, all she could go on was instinct and intuition.

- She would use two or three trusted colleagues as sounding boards.

Alice needed to keep asking herself: 'Am I getting the *real* information I need?' – the whole truth, so to speak.

Many CEOs wilt under the heat of the media spotlight. Alice, as the rare-as-hen's-teeth female CEO of an FTSE-listed company, found it particularly scorching. As well as the usual interest generated by her position, she faced additional scrutiny because of her gender. (The press rarely mentions the dress or appearance of a male CEO, but Alice's every outfit and change of hairstyle was open to comment – often at the expense of what she had said or done.) It can be hard not to take negative press personally, particularly when it concerns personal matters. Her husband found it exceptionally hard not to be hurt when he saw his loved one castigated in the press. Reminding him that today's front page story is tomorrow's chip wrapper did not always help.

Robin Linnecar covers communicating with the media in detail in Chapter 7, but for the purposes of my scenario it is important to acknowledge that, as well as being personally stressful, relentless media attention takes up time the CEO can ill afford to give it. Not only the actual time taken up by interviews, telephone calls, etc., but also the subsequent time expended on fretting and post-mortems. To minimize that latter time, the CEO must get some distance from the harassment and thicken his or her skin! The self-protection measures I suggested to Alice will help any CEO in a similar situation.

- **Buffer your self-confidence.** I stressed to Alice the importance of remembering her many achievements, and suggested that she should keep a log, rather like a journal, of things that had gone well, her major successes, and the things of which she was most proud. Over time, this became an invaluable resource to which she referred when the going got tough. It helped her bounce back from setbacks, and to keep a sense of proportion.

- **Make sure you have a good support mechanism.** Another piece of 'homework' for Alice was to list all her sources of support – people she could confide in. Some CEOs find that their partners can be good sources of support if they are also involved in business, and, indeed, Alice found Iain well able to understand the challenges she faced. But he had his own business to run and, after a hard day at the office, did not want to spend his evenings hearing all about Alice's day! So I encouraged Alice to look at other sources of support, not just people who could empathize with her business persona, but people who valued Alice for herself.

- **Use your friends and family!** Alice identified a number of people with whom she could relax and temporarily forget about Girl. These included her brother, to whom she had been close since childhood, and a couple of close female friends. She resolved to make more time for these people, for her own good as well as their pleasure.

● **Find friends in your working world.** Alice also wanted to find a group of business contacts with whom she could network. She was much more comfortable with small groups than large associations, so she and one of her female friends, a lawyer, decided to create their own networking group. They identified a small number of like-minded contacts and set up quarterly lunches at which Chatham House rules applied. Alice found it very stimulating to talk through some of her business challenges with such a group. She told me she returned from these lunches re-energized.

Invariably during our coaching sessions, the subject of home/work balance raised its head. So how could Alice achieve it? Being disciplined, and recognizing that spending time with family and friends was just as valid a goal in life as any business objective, were the first steps. Once she started to reflect on this, Alice came up with some creative ideas. Here are a few of them:

● Scheduling time for regular exercise every week.

● Going home from work at 5pm on a specified day of the week, and sticking to this.

● Being ruthless about not working on Saturday or Sunday – at least one day every weekend.

● Booking and taking regular holidays.

● Learning some relaxation techniques such as meditation or yoga, and taking quiet time for herself.

● Planning some weekends away with Iain to visit his daughters at university.

Believing that human beings cannot function effectively if they do not take rest and exercise regularly is the cornerstone of this part of the time management equation. No CEO should feel guilty about doing any of the above; they all help with the primary purpose of being an effective CEO and good role model.

Reviewing our work together after several months, Alice was enthusiastic about learning to re-prioritize her time. She still had days when others seemed to demand too much of her attention, but she believed she had made real progress in creating a better work/life balance and in having more time for thinking and planning. She recognized and valued her support – Iain and the girls, her brother, friends, networking group and her invaluable personal assistant. She had developed a greater sense of self-belief and feeling of being in control through this process, and had even learnt to worry less about what the press said about her. The senior team at Girl was shaping up well and once a new chairman was on board, Alice believed she would have more assistance in managing her time but the insight she had gained through our coaching sessions gave her the tools to do so.

Reaching a Resolution

In order to meet the challenge of maximizing his or her value to the organization, with limited and pressurized time, a CEO must tackle the following questions:

- What can I, and only I, do for this organization?
- To whom can I delegate the rest?
- How can I create more thinking time?
- Do I need an effective blocking PA?
- How do I move from professional survival to personal fulfilment?
- How can I control the information flow to what I need, when I need it?
- How can I protect myself from media-induced stress?
- How can I create time for maintaining my own health and well-being?

Let's bring this picture to life!

Chapter 4

Energizing the Organization Through Leadership

Peter Sedgwick

Context

> *'What keeps me awake isn't so much the fear, it's the sheer energy, rush of ideas, impatience, and desire to get things moving. I want my people fired up around my agenda. I want to get them heading in roughly the same direction. In a word – I want them energized! That's a big part of what I think I'm here for.'*

This chapter differs from the others in that it focuses on interventions which involve both one-to-one coaching, and group work that brings together, motivates and, above all, energizes the top team. I will also examine how a leader works with the three crucial agendas – business, group, and personal – negotiates the territory that lies between vision and action, and animates that territory in ways which:

- Energize the whole organization, often through innovative and accelerated means.

- Engage the most important people in the community.

- Facilitate in the leader a personal transition from functional director to transformational leader.

In the specific context of a leader and their organization, 'energizing' means bringing to life each of these three agendas through a series of specific interventions to accelerate the change process at critical points during his or her transition. An energizing leader will quickly develop an acute awareness of what is preoccupying key players at all levels and edges of the organization. He or she will use this to carry people with them, and inspire the organization to share their energy.

The prime time for energizing is before, during and shortly after transition to a senior leadership role. It is particularly appropriate to the leader's transition, because of the scale and complexity of the community and the personal and deliberate shift it involves. This is sometimes described as making the shift from transactional to transformational leadership, insofar as it is not only his or her role the leader must reframe, but also the underlying behaviours and assumptions that go with it. Along the path from strategy to implementation, the energizing performance can be critical in creating a decisive and workable bridge between an informed vision and a well-crafted action programme.

I focus here on coaching and facilitating a CEO-in-waiting and the people around him during critical stages of transition, and describe some of the interventions which helped to bring his agendas to life thereby: energizing his people; demonstrating his transformational leadership capabilities; and positioning him as the successor to the incumbent CEO.

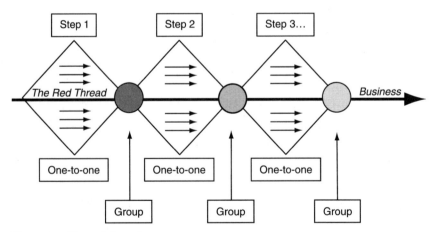

Figure 4.1 *The red thread.*

It can be helpful to imagine the coaching process as a single 'here to there' journey with a series of connected steps.

In Figure 4.1, the continuous line ('The Red Thread') connects alternating individual (one-to-one) and group (one-to-many) interventions: the diamonds form the 'heartbeat' of the process. Correctly gauging sequence, pacing, and timing during a live process which is far less linear is an essential part of the leader–coach dialogue.

Group interventions – which bring together the leader's three agendas – are held at critical points along the journey. They are important tests of the leader's personal development, and can greatly accelerate business change. They don't just happen, though. Apart from the meticulous contracting with both individual and group at every step, a coach engages key people in the leader's community before and often after each event. In facilitating the group, the coach holds the red thread (what the leader has formally said he or she wants) while creatively engaging the collective brain-power and energy of the group.

The coach will often arrange for the client, and sometimes their group, to meet outside the normal setting in order to foster an atmosphere different from the usual working one, and encourage innovative thinking. In the case of interventions that last for more than a day, well-conceived social activities will help to develop informal relationships and team spirit.

The quality of the settings for group events often has a decisive influence on the outcome. It is therefore essential to choose venues with enormous care, considering location, accessibility, atmosphere and quality of space, and always bearing in mind the balance you wish to strike between a different environment and a comfortable (or, indeed, challenging) one.

A crucial factor in the success of these events will be the leader's own courage, capacity and appetite to make a personal commitment of time and energy – having the will and discipline to set each agenda with the coach and follow through with key groups. Alongside one-to-one coaching, well-timed energizing events with key members of the leader's community can, and do, have a decisive impact on bringing his or her agenda to life. Their design and delivery require substantial commitment and painstaking preparation but can accelerate the change process and, in fact, create space for the leader to do other things.

In creating such interventions, I have found it useful to remember a long-standing prescription for good architecture: 'commodity, firmness, and delight'. They should be useful and will be well-structured but without the element of delight they will be less than complete. Any formulaic approach, method or tool set can be applied only to a limited extent in designing such interventions, but the scenario that follows will provide useful guidance.

The Company

Global Services Group (GSG) had existed for less than four years and embraced a large number of entities from around the world: more than 100,000 employees across over 50 countries. English was the native language of less than 25% of the workforce. It comprised five core businesses with a European head office and a strong European cultural mix at senior levels. Its revenue was equivalent to €15 billion in 2000. It was a fast, hands-on group with synergies across the businesses and a traditional management board + supervisory (non-executive) board structure.

The Client

Roland Peterson was a 45-year-old continental European, married with three children. His early career had been as a big-five accountant. He had held a series of financial director roles in international blue-chip companies in different sectors. At the time of our work together he had been finance director and chief financial officer for three years.

The Challenge

'My ambition is simple; I want to be CEO of this company. This is my landmark.'

Roland's overarching ambition was to create an agenda that would serve as a platform for a future bid to become CEO. I will focus here on what he did to energize – make a decisive impact on – the key communities through which he could set the direction of the business and shape his own future.

When we first met, his immediate challenge was putting Finance in shape – energizing his global finance directors to create and deliver a programme to get the finance basics right and embed a stretching vision that would impact the whole business. From this arose a unique combination of personal coaching and group interventions.

The challenge was then amplified in two dramatic steps:

- GSG's main board was reconfigured to support a divisionally-led business. This prompted another series of group interventions, as a result of which a wider business transformation agenda emerged in which the CFO had a key role.

- Roland was then appointed fundamentally to re-shape the Corporate Centre – at the same time as keeping the finance programme running and initiating a series of ambitious strategic projects. It was critical that he should energize future leaders – 'high potentials' – around the changes.

From the beginning, we acknowledged the risks as well as the rewards of the journey ahead, especially when working 'against the grain' – trying out new ideas and questioning old ways. We also agreed that we had to inject a great deal of fun into the process – too often a missing ingredient in corporate and personal transformation!

The Desired Results

- Preparing Roland for a CEO role.
- Ensuring that Roland set that business agenda and launched the major initiatives to achieve it.
- Energizing Roland's community to work with him.
- Articulating and achieving his personal vision and agenda.

The Developing Approach

I became involved with Roland in far from ideal circumstances: with almost no notice, and never having met him before, I was asked to design and lead a two-day meeting for 20 of his finance directors (FDs). Its purpose was to create an actionable agenda around Roland's vision for transforming Finance and to bring that agenda to life so that the group would be engaged. The briefing indicated several potential points for success, but showed that the situation was potentially fraught with difficulty.

The Preferred Conditions for Designing Such an Event

- Extensive one-to-one preparation with the client and his key people.
- Evidence of a direct, decisive, and highly committed client.
- Confidence in the group's capabilities and participation.
- A good and known venue.

The Known Situation for this Event

- Because GSG was a conglomeration of many formerly independent companies, there were many legacy finance functions.
- It would be a large international group with language barriers and national culture differences.
- This was a newly formed group with no built-up trust.

- I had no idea of how positive (or negative) their response to change was.

- I would meet the client for the first time only an hour before the event due to start, and had not previously met any member of his team.

It sounded to me as if Roland were dealing with the modern-day equivalent of feuding feudal barons. (In fact, Roland, too, saw this parallel and requested a medieval banquet for the second evening!)

The First Evening

This, as always, was a rapid and very revealing induction. The conversations and body language of the group's members indicated their unfamiliarity with each other, and their deep desire to protect their own areas. It was an uneasy gathering, but many were affected by Roland's charisma. When greeting them he managed to blend the personal and the professional, creating an atmosphere of one-to-one intimacy by 'working' the room and making sure that he had a personal word for each participant, and stressing the business's need for excellence in his welcoming speech.

Day One

Simple metaphor and image are powerful, especially with mixed-language groups. On the first morning I described the meeting agenda in terms of a 'here-to-there' bridge. I then described the agenda we would use to build that bridge:

Day One – 'Where do We Want to Be?'

- Roland to present his vision for the future.

- Identify what each leader can contribute.

- An assessment of where we are now.

- Generate ideas about what will make the vision a reality.

Day Two – Turn the 'What?' into the 'How?'

- Revisit recombine ideas to make vision a reality.

- Test and refine the key areas to act on.

- Agree the structure and programme for a route forward.

- Individuals signal commitment by signing up to deliver specific actions.

After Roland had presented his vision, we conducted a thorough assessment of the participants' expectations and potential contributions. Then, to define the starting point, there was 'no holds barred' evaluation of the business from a top City analyst and two leading thinkers on business transformation (one with the theory, the other with the experience).

The main process of the day revolved around mapping what could be done to achieve the vision. The participants wrote notes on small pieces of paper detailing their ideas. As they were doing so, conversation sparked further thought. The work was done individually, in small groups and in plenary. The notes were put on the wall for the whole group to see and discuss.

By the time we finished for the day, the 20 had constructed a highly graphic view of the bridge itself: a 10-metre long story-wall covered with over 500 ideas that detailed what Roland's group might have to do to cross it.

The group discussions were not, as I had forewarned Roland, without frustration and conflict. This was the price of a process which stretched the group and forced its members to tackle directly the latent differences between them. (At one point Roland passed me a note asking: 'are the guys from the UK really meant to be banging the table like that?!'.) Still, it soon became clear that constant and full participation across the board, and very direct, open expression of ideas suited Roland's style.

The medieval banquet was a resounding success, largely due to Roland's bonhomie. He inspired a relaxed 'party' environment in which traditional 'enemies' began to break down the barriers and see that it would be possible to work as a team.

Day Two

The tone of the second day was very different. The group members were now comfortable working together, building on each others' ideas, and robust discussion, and able to meet Roland's frequent challenges to convert the 'what' to 'how'. The bridge began to assume structure as the ideas were re-visited, re-combined, expanded once more and finally ordered into a powerful blueprint made up of a dozen clear action areas.

It was an extraordinary achievement that, by 5pm on that second and final day signatures and dates for delivery had been added to each of these, publicly declaring the group's shared commitment. We agreed to hold a 'part two' meeting just eight weeks later.

As Roland shook hands with every one of the exhausted, but exhilarated participants before leaving for the airport, it was clear that his relationship with them had undergone a huge shift during the meeting. He had what he wanted and I had a clear mandate to work with them again.

Review

At our first formal one-to-one meeting the following week Roland showed me a picture that had been drawn during the group session. It depicted a confident-looking figure, unwittingly approaching the edge of a cliff: 'Now we know the magic and power of the "event". It energizes, commits and sets out the tracks ... Next I need to know how to sustain this energy so I can keep that guy away from the cliff-edge – or give him wings.' The success of the 48-hour event marked a significant change in our relationship and set the scene for the next step.

Negotiating New Terrain

Ten weeks later at another one-to-one meeting Roland announced:
'GSG will be re-organized around a divisional structure and the
board composition will change to reflect that. The new board and
the level below it need to work through the consequences. How can
we work together on this? We have just seven days.'

This was a seismic shift in the business terrain. He had recently
been appointed board director responsible for the Group Corporate
Centre (in addition to his other functions), and saw that this
part of his agenda was now moving to the fore. This was shortly
after the second of the FD meetings and another event-driven
conversation began to take shape. I was beginning to understand
the pattern emerging in each strand of Roland's development path:

● Business agenda: getting finance in shape (creating a legacy)
  while sponsoring new strategic initiatives to transform the
  business (changing the world) – more usually the domain of the
  CEO.

● Community agenda: engaging the members through whom the
  business agenda could be achieved by a very direct use of group
  interventions.

● Personal agenda: Roland's ambition to become CEO.

This latest structural change set a new challenge to all these agendas.
The board was one of Roland's closest communities – as was the
level below the board, the 60 directors on whom the change would
have the most immediate impact. Many of these leaders would form
the newly empowered divisional boards. A different dynamic was
emerging and Roland would be both participant in and shaper of
the changed leadership structure.

Roland briefed me on the issues involved and, in spite of the limits
of geography and time, the wonders of virtual communication
enabled me to consult closely with each board member and, with
their input, I selected internal facilitators to support divisional
work.

My proposal was ambitious: an event with the new board and the 60 directors, a day-and-a-half long, the following weekend in Lausanne. At this point, one of Roland's most trusted confidantes entered into the dialogue: Marcus Ericson was a business unit leader who worked closely with the incumbent CEO. He was also a former boss of Roland's, and a highly creative and experienced fixer. He seemed unruffled – even energized – by the sheer logistical challenge of gathering GSG executives at short notice from around the world for a full and highly participative working weekend. The design was agreed.

It was an enormous relief to go through the process with full preparation and the declared engagement of the client, and I felt far more confident of success than I had before our previous event.

The event I facilitated and the CEO led included elements of the earlier FD meetings adapted for a much larger group, but this time the stakes were higher, the tribal differences far greater, and Roland was as much participant as owner. It was significant that Roland, Marcus and I organized this event and pre-planned its content before in close collaboration with the CEO.

On the first evening the CEO concluded his presentation of the new structure with a set of short- and medium-term targets and expectations for each of his new board members. I outlined the working process for the event. Working to one huge story-wall which covered all four walls of an aircraft hangar-sized space, each of the 60 board members took charge of his or her own new team and began to construct his or her own division's 'here-to-there' path. Mapping this path – and then aligning it with each of the other divisions' – was to be 'the main course' of this first session.

Views were inevitably divergent and tension and dissent were often close to the surface. Dealing with this there and then was a challenging first test of each board member's leadership and commitment. I deliberately punctuated this core process with a number of parallel strands designed to inform, create competition and bring thorny issues to the surface. For instance:

1. Presentations from notables including international statesmen and business experts.

2. Challenging exercises in which the separate 'tribes' had to work together, such as smaller teams crossing a 'minefield' using only non-verbal communication

What was noticeable – in addition to the very high quality of presented results – was a marked shift in the larger group's capacity and will to work together on the new business agenda.

When the time came for relaxation, we created evening environments and activities that made a visible difference in building informal links between the 60. (The most dramatic was a 'Hollywood' dinner cruise of Lac Leman during which groups presented films they had made during the day aided by actors, look-alikes and the full paraphernalia of a big-budget production team, right down to wardrobe and makeup.) But there was still a long way to go!

Back to the Personal Agenda

While these group interventions were unfolding, I had begun to have more regular one-to-one coaching conversations with Roland. In these sessions Roland explored and tested his ambitions and business agendas in more depth. This was probably the closest the coaching came to a formal process, with me mostly listening, sometimes prompting with open questions, and occasionally challenging very directly. During this time, many of the preoccupations and development issues that would define his subsequent career began to emerge. He had needed the earlier group meetings to build a degree of trust and respect – and shared risk – from which we could work.

We charted (literally) the story so far, exploring not just the highs and lows of the past but also how the future might look. We projected three years into the future – the earliest he thought he might be promoted to CEO – and discussed how he could use the business agenda to promote his personal one:

- Develop a strategy to reshape the Corporate Centre.

- Energize the Corporate Centre's 30 high potentials.

- Choose a core team of Corporate Centre directors and develop their leadership skills and ability to work together.

Reshaping and Securing the Corporate Centre

On the underside of the cigar box a neatly hand-written series of bullet points framed the answer to my question about what Roland wanted from his Corporate Centre – a stylish non-UK variant to the 'back of a cigarette packet' scribble.

Roland wanted a Corporate Centre that:

- Would be best-in-class.

- Had transparent and stretching performance targets.

- Would be a great place to work.

Having nurtured the finance community to deliver his change programme (at our first event), and strengthened his credentials within the re-shaped board (through the CEO's participation in the second event), Roland's next challenge was to put the Corporate Centre in order. In an organization committed to devolving power to its business units it would have to be demonstrably more than a simple spring clean.

I had challenged Roland about where his time would go now the agenda was becoming fuller and increasingly complex. His PA regularly mused about the current diary: 'it's around 268% full today – and rising!' It was time to confront a growing polarization between the immediate 'basics' that would form the 'must-do' part of his role versus the growing portfolio of higher-risk strategic projects which could potentially transform the business – and its share price. Roland's fast brain and predilection for deal-shaping meant that he could be pulled too strongly in one direction. Roland acknowledged the Faustian bargain to be struck here: the only way to create the time and space for 'the big stuff' was to have in place a strong infrastructure. Heather Dawson examined this bargain closely in Chapter 1.

The burning question was how to drive a tough set of changes in the Corporate Centre while retaining the goodwill and delivery of this local community and still leave time and space to explore a growing portfolio of strategic projects. The main focus for our continuing discussions was the project he would sponsor, with leadership from Magnus, to re-shape the Corporate Centre. It is tougher to achieve your ambitions through consensus than coercion, but both Roland and Magnus preferred the former course.

Another set of group interventions began to take shape, and I designed a two-day meeting for 30 people who were, by the Corporate Centre's own estimation, the top movers and shakers. Over the course of this event they would be developed to play important parts in the change process, which would help to provide a future generation of leaders in the re-shaped Centre. We agreed that Roland would invite the 30, but not take part.

The meeting took place at Helsingor, Denmark – a long way from home.

I held a series of small meetings to learn the current perceptions of the business and assess the extent of hopes and fears the change might bring. I then constructed a highly participative agenda around the development of management skills to enable the future Centre to excel. It was deliberately simplistic: this was an extremely functional, bright, multi-cultural group, average age 35, and a formal structure was expected, if only as a starting point from which they could shape the event for themselves.

Early on, members of the group started to acknowledge collectively for the first time that their world was changing in ways which would personally affect most of them. During an exercise about customer intimacy, their underlying anger, frustration and sense of betrayal began to eclipse the formal agenda. I told them about a picture a coaching colleague has on her office wall, knowing that it would have particular resonance with this Northern European group. It shows people talking around a table, oblivious to an enormous and angry-looking moose beneath it which is beginning to stir and will inevitably upset it when he does. Depicting their resentment in this way helped to diffuse the situation in the moment, but deeper action was essential.

At this point, with some re-contracting, the agenda was modified to allow time and space for them to release their negative feelings and thereby begin to diffuse them. When we broke for dinner, we took part in an extraordinarily animated round of story telling and performances on themes of personal change. Most of the group learned more about each other in a few hours than they had in months of working together at the Corporate Centre.

The following morning, we entered once more into a formal agenda, this time around business processes. They were still far from acknowledging that there was anything they could do to influence their own futures, and the atmosphere was tense. By 10am it was time to intervene and through an interjection of controlled anger (a risky and rarely used shock tactic that should be employed only after deep thought), I confronted them head-on with their passivity – they were leaders, after all. This achieved a decisive shift in the group's self-perception and energy. For the next three hours, a more-or-less self-organizing group took the first tentative steps towards mapping and shaping its own future. It was by no means a full resolution, but by 4pm the group had a set of actions to take home.

The final 90 minutes were devoted to a closing team exercise on the beach, involving five truck-loads of building sand, a lot of wooden form-work, a large number of shovels, and three teams of 10. The results amazed the teams not to mention the bemused Danish passers-by who knew they were witnessing something rather unusual! The group's newly released creative energy had taken physical form in a series of remarkable sand sculptures, which depicted its collective vision for a better future.

Developing the Core Team

Six months after the Corporate Centre re-design had been implemented, I took Roland and his relatively new team of five Corporate Centre directors for two days together, well away from the Centre, to develop individual leadership skills. It had been Roland's idea ('the soft stuff's always the hardest, right?!') and had taken six weeks of diary creativity to organize. Nevertheless, on a beautiful late spring evening Roland and his team all arrived at the small spa town near Vienna where we were to spend the next two days and nights.

By now, Roland had made great progress in creating a stronger finance community, introducing new thinking and best-in-class practices, from board level down, on financial performance, and re-shaping the Corporate Centre. In addition he had dozens of other projects and potential 'deals' in the pipeline, some of which could dramatically re-shape GSG's portfolio and overall value.

One of Roland's aims had been to delegate many of his CFO functions to a small cadre of highly capable and trusted directors, each of whom I had supported in leading projects to implement the Corporate Centre transition. Afterwards, we had extended the development stretch by each of the team taking on an important new position which did not necessarily play to his or her proven strengths. As well as fostering individual growth, it might help shape potential successors.

They all felt it was time to review their progress, strengthen their relationships with each other, and spend time developing and testing skills they now knew were necessary in leading the new Corporate Centre. These were the key ingredients of Roland's Vienna agenda.

Within minutes of arriving, the restrained formality of the eighteenth-century dining room was shattered by a hugely open and animated series of conversations that began to engage head-on some of the more sensitive issues that lay behind our agenda. It was more like a rowdy family re-union than a business group, and the polar opposite of any GSG group I had encountered before the interventions. This was crucial to the success of the very intense and personal work planned for the event, which would require a mature group with a significant level of trust.

Over the preceding six months, I had worked with them individually and as a group to chart the leadership behaviours and values that matched the new context at GSG. They had begun to relate their own strengths and development needs to this leadership map. My team for the two days included a coaching colleague who, on the first evening and morning, provided the participants with results from a series of diagnostics I had asked them to complete in advance – Myers–Briggs Type Indictor and Kolb's Learning Style Questionnaire. These diagnostics are designed to:

● Unearth different styles of working and thinking within the group.

● Raise awareness of both personal and group preferences in working and thinking.

● Promote acceptance of diversity within the team.

● Build a common leadership vocabulary.

Working through them is a revealing and personally challenging process, so I added to the mix two actors who would support my work by bringing to life the leadership situations we were working with.

The structure of the intervention was not complex, though the actual dynamics of what amounted to group coaching sessions were far from simple. Once they were equipped with the results of the diagnostics, they worked in groups of varying sizes for the rest of the day and most of the following morning. The challenge was to give each participant time and space to re-create the real work situations he or she had identified beforehand. It was demanding work but I exploited the unique setting to give full rein to the creative energy and fun which were becoming distinctive parts of group work with Roland and his people.

Amidst laughter, openness and heartfelt 'a-*ha*'s their differences became a strength – now that they were in the open – as well as a continuing challenge which would not be resolved in 48 hours. Nevertheless, the whole exercise was very highly rated by all the participants – as well as their people who later commented on noticeable improvements in behaviours. The day after, Roland approved a similar programme for everyone at the senior level below this leadership group.

Landmark Reached: Re-set the Compass

> '*It was in the national newspapers almost as quickly as word got out internally. He's gone. GSG needs a new CEO*'.

The incumbent CEO's departure took everybody, including Roland, by surprise. Roland's bid for the job would succeed or fail on the reputation he had already established at key points in his community. Our work together had ensured that his three agendas were now congruent and his people energized – working well with him and each other. Following the red thread, Roland had demonstrated his capability as a transformational leader. He had transformed his people by energizing them and creating and exemplary infrastructure.

This had made Roland an obvious candidate for the CEO position, which he was offered and accepted. Now it was time to use what he had learned about energizing his extended CFO community on the entire company … .

Reaching a Resolution

● How do you rate your commitment and ability to energize the business and the people on whom your own success depends?

● Can you define your wants around your personal, community and business agendas?

● What are your plans to bring these agendas to life – and just how ambitious and innovative are they? What can you make happen within the next 12 weeks, for instance?

● What are your default responses – the patterns which have helped or hindered your biggest life and career achievements to date?

● Who do you surround yourself with? Are they the people you need to support, challenge and succeed you?

● What time will you spend off-line this year with your board – and with the 20 or so most valuable people below board level?

● How do you take reality checks – what time and space do you create for reflection?

● Who, outside the business, do you trust to partner and challenge you – and what contract have you formed (or will you form) with them to support your journey?

● Is it working, is it fun, can you see, hear, smell and touch the energy!?

Ah, now this is paradise.

Chapter 5

Delivering Strategy Through the Top Team

Sue Godfrey

Context

Changes in the dynamics by which businesses operate have never been so dramatic. As Peninah Thomson explained in the Introduction, events and technological developments in the new millennium have brought into true focus the extent and interconnected nature of the global economy, and the speed at which companies are expected to respond is far greater than before. The quality and style of leadership in such times are critical to success.

Many CEOs spend their time working on the strategic agendas of their firms: monitoring the external environment, interfacing with the investment community and anticipating how they can meet their needs. Most CEOs have strong ambitions, dreams for the future, and a sense of how they will win in their market places – but their prime concern is to provide focus, direction and, above all, a successful strategy. Their strategy will not be fully realized if they underestimate the importance of motivating the leaders of their organizations and delivering results through people.

Realization of the corporate dream relies on the quality of leadership demonstrated not only by CEOs, but also – in a large organization – by the top 1% of their workforce. To retain a place in the premier league, firms need appropriate leadership benchstrength. When looking at the development of the firm there is a substantial challenge to provide the senior executive resources needed to fulfil the strategic objectives. Linking business strategy and people strategy to deliver results can give an organization a competitive edge.

In this chapter I will focus on this vital factor in any company's success, discussing how CEOs can:

- Assess the leadership capability in their organizations, and look for gaps.
- Install a systematic process of key talent management.
- Develop their top team.

The pool of managerial talent is often the result of many and varied changes, rather than a systematic and forward-looking process of HR planning for the needs of the business. A large number of companies are now the products of many years of evolution, over which process re-engineering has been used to achieve bottom-line efficiency or speed to market, and mergers and acquisitions to structure top-line growth. The traditional structures have been transformed and people are now expected to work in multi-disciplinary teams, often matrixed across functions and geography.

This has required the leaders to develop new core competencies (which some may have while others may not have acquired).

In this chapter, which differs from all others except Chapter 8 in that it deals with a real and named company, Glaxo Wellcome (GW), I will examine groundbreaking work in taking a systematic approach to developing its top team according to strategic require-ments. This work took place from 1995 to 2000, prior to GW's merger with SmithKline, and, while it did not involve coaching the CEO, it was undertaken as a result of his instructions.

Although this chapter refers specifically refer to a large multi-national company, the processes involved – and the manner of their execution – can easily be adapted to develop the top team of any company, whatever its size, to align with its strategic agenda. The principles remain the same.

In 1995 the outlook for GW was bleak as a result of the loss of patents and the introduction of generic competition. The US market alone (which represented the majority of GW's total market) expected revenue losses of $1 billion for 1997. The challenge was created in the United States to 'zip the dip' between required revenue and projected income and protect the company's share price. And it wasn't just the United States – all markets needed to make their contributions to grow revenues and maintain profit margins if GW were to succeed in delivering its promise to the investors, which was to achieve flat earnings in the years 1996–1998 and deliver double-digit growth from 1999. While significant investment in research and development would play its part, investment in people was also crucial at this stage.

Sir Richard Sykes, Chairman and Chief Executive, recognized that a transformation was needed if the company were to maintain its superior market position. As you can see from Figure 5.1 overleaf, 30% of revenues were now coming from new product introductions.

GW was a wealthy company but even after process re-engineering had not achieved bottom-line efficiency. There was still room for improvement. The company also faced the inevitable challenges associated with its rapid growth from the mid-1980s to mid-1990s and its recent merger. The former had resulted in an over-stretched and, in many cases, under-developed workforce. The latter had caused redundancies, uncertainty and a consequent tendency to focus on job retention issues rather than on the markets outside. In this climate of cutting out duplication, there was resentment between ex-Glaxo and ex-Wellcome employees, which led to a damaging failure to share information and learning. Breaking down these legacy silos and fostering a culture of co-operation would be a crucial element of the programme.

Now GW needed to move from a local and devolved structure to one that acknowledged the global market place. It wanted to be both global and local. There was a strong desire to build a distributed entrepreneurial culture that would encourage the transfer of

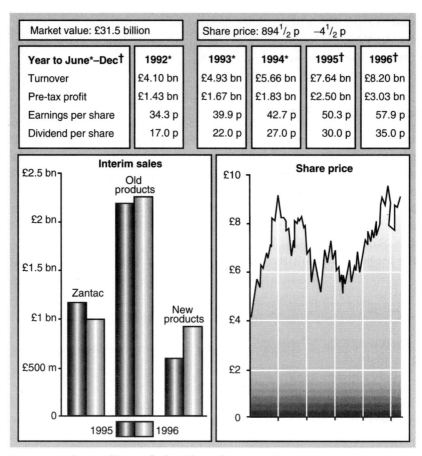

Year to June*–Dec†	1992*	1993*	1994*	1995†	1996†
Turnover	£4.10 bn	£4.93 bn	£5.66 bn	£7.64 bn	£8.20 bn
Pre-tax profit	£1.43 bn	£1.67 bn	£1.83 bn	£2.50 bn	£3.03 bn
Earnings per share	34.3 p	39.9 p	42.7 p	50.3 p	57.9 p
Dividend per share	17.0 p	22.0 p	27.0 p	30.0 p	35.0 p

Market value: £31.5 billion   Share price: 894 1/2 p   –4 1/2 p

Figure 5.1 *Glaxo Wellcome. © The Telegraph Group Ltd 1996/1997.*

learning across boundaries to be able to leverage economies of scale for global benefit. GW was known by investors for its strong cash generation, and needed to keep that reputation by ensuring profit with all growth.

In 1995, the company knew that to maintain its competitiveness it needed to invest in the period 1996–1998 which would lead to a short-term diminution of margins but that this would result in a return to double-digit growth by 1999. The strategic focus was to release the potential of markets around the world and achieve 'Big Hairy Audacious Goals' (BHAGs): a transformational step change in the way the company did business.[1]

Client Company Profile

Glaxo Wellcome, one of the world's leading pharmaceuticals companies, was formed in 1995 from the integration of Glaxo Plc and Wellcome Plc. It was headquartered in the UK and employed 54,000 people in 76 operating companies world-wide, with manufacturing in more than 50 countries and supplies reaching over 150 markets. Seven of the world's 40 best-selling medicines were from the GW stable. Sales revenues in 1997 were £7.98 billion with a 5% share of the fragmented global market.

The Challenge

Sir Richard Sykes articulated the elements of the challenge very clearly in 1995.

> 'We're in business to make money. But I don't see that as the number one priority; the number one priority is to get the business right ... Strong leadership, good people, good product flow, bringing value to patients throughout the world ... If you get those right, then everything else will fall into place.'

From the 1990s GW invested over £1 billion a year in the research and development of new products. Cost-cutting caused by a change in the US market – the increasing domination of managed care as opposed to reactive medicine (keeping people healthy rather than treating them when they ceased to be) – had led to a decline in profits.

The company needed to retain its profit margin to satisfy the demands of investors, who wanted a long-term strategy founded on the introduction of new products. With the imminent expiry of patents on blockbusters like Glaxo's Zantac and Wellcome's Zovirax, and huge increases in the costs of research and development (particularly in the emergent biotechnology field), the race for product innovation was on.

What would these challenges demand of GW and its leaders?

- Entrepreneurship.
- Fostering a culture of innovation.
- A high degree of comfort with ambiguity.
- Continuous individual and group learning.
- Learning across the boundaries of functions, regions and nations.
- Outrunning the pace of change.
- Sharp focus on delivering the business's demands.

To meet them Sir Richard requested a programme to develop GW's top 300 leaders. Its aim was to build a cadre of executives who would respond to those challenges. I was appointed to a new role to help Sir Richard achieve his ambition. At that time, GW did not have the capability to develop a programme to meet these challenges, so I followed a revolutionary course to do so with a range of outside partners.

The Desired Results

- To create a coherent leadership framework aligned to the strategic imperatives and values of the firm.
- To assess executives and review with them their leadership capabilities.
- To develop the people who would, over a three-year period, provide sufficient entrepreneurial input to bridge the gap in revenues caused by the expiry of patent on blockbuster drugs.
- To design interventions that would shift the culture to allow each executive to take responsibility for releasing the potential in the market place.

- To create and embed a set of processes for key talent management.

- To connect people, encouraging executives to learn from and with others, to enable learning to flow across boundaries

The Developing Approach

In 1995 following a top-team conference to look at strategy, Sir Richard Sykes commissioned a series of corporate action programmes to build the business and deliver his promises to the investment community. One was designed to develop the senior leadership cadre to enable it to release the organization's potential. Sir Richard believed that the entrepreneurial opportunity was available in the market place and he needed to inspire his people to grab it.

The Executive Committee of the Plc board initiated the Senior Executive Development Programme (SEDP). A task force of senior line executives and human resources staff identified a series of action steps to grow the leadership capability of the firm and deliver our promise to the investment community: these are shown in the Desired Results section above.

We then drew up a project timetable:

- November 1995: communicate the SEDP and involve key stakeholders.

- March–July 1996: determine the leadership capabilities required to achieve business goals.

- July–December 1996: design a leadership framework.

- March–September 1996: find and assess key talent.

- September 1996: embed key talent process.

- January 1997–October 1998: deliver the SEDP.

- April 1998: continuously cascade the learning through conferences and alumni groups.

Finding Partners to Create and Deliver the SEDP

The first job was to select partners. I was looking for a high-profile business school, which could relate to our corporate agenda and work with me to design something that very bright executives who hadn't had much formal business education would find engaging. I drew up a short-list from the leagues of schools regarded highly for their ability to deliver company-specific executive education.

My preliminary enquiries revealed that the idea of rolling out a programme quickly was heresy: the normal lead-time was about 18 months. We needed to have something in place much sooner, ideally to have it *delivered* within 18 months, as our revenues were already under threat. None of the schools was interested in delivering 10+ programmes in 18 months – a huge time commitment for them. I was asking the faculty to be available for 5–10 days per month, to be dedicated to the fast rollout of the programme. For the investment to deliver its value we needed to create critical mass within the organization, fast. It also emerged that many of the schools were not interested in delivering a bespoke product.

I eventually decided to approach three schools: the Fuqua School of Business at Duke University (USA), INSEAD (France) and the London Business School (UK). I asked if they would be prepared to work with me and, more importantly, with each other, to design and deliver a programme within the specified timeframe.

I chose these three schools partly because of GW's enormous size and global nature, which it was desirable to reflect by using schools which were in different countries but close enough together for communication and travel to be easy. I was also aware that each of them had relevant specialties in terms of faculty.

- The London Business School was close to GW's headquarters in England. I wanted to be able to call on Professor John Stopford's wisdom in strategic planning and the School's highly regarded work in inspiring entrepreneurship.

- Fuqua was in the same city as GW's US head office and, since it represented such a huge proportion of GW's market, learning to win in the USA would be paramount. I also wanted to harness Professor Blair Sheppard's expertise in understanding and creating corporate trust, and the school's famed teaching in the area of creating innovation culture.

- INSEAD was a leading business school in continental Europe. Professor Yves Doz was renowned for his knowledge and teaching of strategy, alliances and, most importantly for our purposes, entrepreneurship in multinational corporations.

The schools liked their freedom and independence, and it was a challenge to them to suggest that GW employees would play a part in design and delivery of the programme. I also wanted to include external coaches and facilitators in the design and rollout, and found that the schools were not used to working with other professional developers.

Our partnership was different from anything these schools had previously undertaken. Working internationally, we would need to agree common terms and contracts, and the three schools – usually fiercely competitive – would need to work collaboratively. Remarkably, all three agreed to move forward with the venture!

The business development teams from the three schools worked hard to iron out the contractual difficulties of bringing three governance structures together. Each school chose a group to work on the project, and a team was brought together to design and deliver the programme. There were a number of significant challenges to overcome:

- Creating fair and equitable reward for faculty from three business schools.

- Asking faculty to team teach to enable consistent quality of delivery.

- Working faster than the normal pace of business schools to deliver 10 programmes over 18 months.

- Building communication with a diverse group of people with differing mental models across many organizations: Faculty from three schools; business school administrators; internal facilitators; external facilitators; five external coaching providers to create global reach; internal stakeholders (CEO, executive directors, steering group, 300 participants).

Creating the Initial Design and Stakeholder Consultation

With the external partners in place, I focused internally to engage the potential participants and involve a group of GW movers and shakers in the design of the programme. I knew that a number of GW's high flyers from around the world had just finished projects to integrate Glaxo and Wellcome. The executive team wanted to keep these people involved in important corporate projects in addition to their day jobs. Their recent integration work would have given them a fresh understanding of the challenges implicit in merging disparate groups and turning competitors into collaborators. They would also have gained insights into the feelings and mood of people within the organization, and honed their skills in dealing with them.

A group of these people formed the steering team chaired by an executive director, Jacques Lapointe, who – in addition to his board responsibilities – ran the UK, South African and Irish commercial businesses. This gave the programme the essential senior-level sponsorship. The team comprised representatives of the global organization's functions and regions, chosen for their demonstrable ability to drive integration. A series of workshop-style meetings created a sense of mutual involvement, elicited useful ideas and dialogue, and enabled us to review and tweak the programme's design as it progressed.

After each meeting there was a report to the board.

The steering team was quickly motivated and involved, but I needed to ensure that we captured the hearts and minds of the key stakeholder and influencers. There was a high risk of the project being derailed by senior executives who just didn't want to 'go back to school'. Buy-in was achieved by a combination of clear sponsorship from the top, and stakeholder involvement in every stage of both design and implementation.

Defining the Leadership Criteria

The full team met only three times at key milestones. Firstly, to agree the protocol for determining the business challenges and how we would identify the leadership capabilities needed. The team also agreed the key stakeholders and personally committed to communicate our intentions to their local businesses.

The executives were unanimous in saying that the company needed to articulate a leadership framework which could be easily understood by all and provide a common style and language. There were discontinuities in the market place caused by the impact of concurrent changes in technology and consumer perspective combined with the ever-changing economic, social and political environments.

When asked what leadership criteria they thought would address these, they suggested:

● Networking and relationship building.

● Managing without boundaries and across borders.

● Working beyond conventional limits.

● Encouraging exploration and originality in all spheres of the business.

● Releasing the potential of others though supporting, coaching and enabling.

At its second meeting the steering team reviewed the findings from the diagnostic phase and signed-off the leadership criteria, which revealed that a leader of GW at that time needed to be a person of parts: four people rolled into one!

● **The Entrepreneur:** GW needed to develop local markets for its full product range, using its entire global strength in a more pro-active and sophisticated way by exploiting opportunities in local markets. An entrepreneurial approach would determine the course of business development and its degree of penetration into new markets. There was a need to manage risks and to do things that were 'unconventional'. The leaders needed to celebrate success and encourage commercially sound experimentation, even if it resulted in failure. As leaders, executives needed to be visionaries and to inspire lateral thinking by creating a climate that fostered bright ideas.

- **The Strategist:** in a vast and very devolved multinational company, leaders needed to apply local strategies to the global context, and to manage complex portfolios within the framework of industry changes in markets, decision makers and customer demands. They needed to be able to see the bigger picture, scan the external environment and influence the direction of healthcare.

- **The Integrator:** to ensure the best possible results, the leaders should be people who could use all branches of the global company as sources of ideas, and build relationships with their equivalents around the world. To that end a significant part of the design was very consciously to engender trusting relationships between executives who would not normally meet as they worked in different countries and, more importantly, functions. It was incumbent on the delivery team to bring peers together and create a climate where relationships could be built on trust. This would streamline the decision-making processes and enable the executives to work beyond their self-constructed boundaries for the greater good of the corporation.

- **The Leader:** a level of personal excellence was required that would engender the same in others, energizing and empowering – releasing the full potential of the organization. This was a company and an industry based on innovation and the creative processes of scientific discovery. Leaders in all areas of the business, not just the scientific, needed to foster and create the appropriate culture. It was business-critical to get new products documented quickly in the regulatory arena, to rationalize using common platforms in manufacturing, and to use existing resources rather than reinventing the wheel in the commercial sector.

Defining the Leadership Framework

We designed a survey based on the defined criteria, which a wider group of executives used to assess their leaders. Its results were analysed and presented to a senior leadership conference for further stakeholder endorsement. The survey revealed that GW had four levers of leadership: reach, trust, self-discipline and support.

With a study of the current thinking about leadership in entre-preneurial organizations,[2] and the help of Professors Stopford (LBS), Sheppard (Fuqua) and Doz (INSEAD), and Dr David Findley (GW Director of Executive Organizational Development), links were made between the business strategy and the leadership profile, and a framework was developed. This framework would help GW's top people to harness the levers of leadership by:

- Encouraging them to **reach** out to the potential in the market place.

- Fostering company-wide relationships built on **trust**.

- Allowing **self-discipline** and determination rather than imposing the traditional command and control structure.

- Creating built-in peer and organizational **support**.

Reviewing and Piloting the Design

At its third and final meeting the design and selection criteria for participants were presented to the steering team. The design of the programme was novel. Rather than using the external environment as the backdrop to internal issues, GW was the primary case study for the programme. Conceptual models were introduced to the design to stimulate thinking, facilitate learning and guide actions. The steering team recommended that the executive members of the board should experience the proposed content of the programme in a pilot workshop, since they needed to endorse this significant investment. The executive board then participated in the first programme and gave feedback for the rollout to the top 300 executives.

The participating executives were involved with faculty in the design, meaning that they were 'owners' of the learning experience (see Figure 5.2).

SEDP Project Plan

Module One

In Module One of the SEDP 30 senior executives at a time went to one of the three business schools for a week for an overview of the SEDP and intensive learning about GW's strategic agenda and the leadership competencies. The time was divided into plenary sessions, small group learning sets, individual reflection and informal socializing. Each learning set had a professional coach both

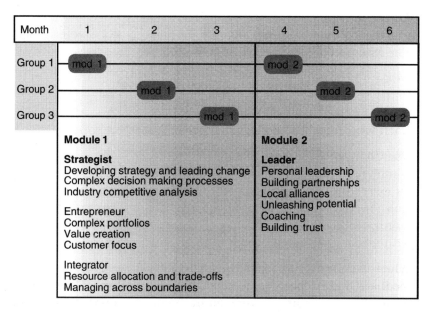

Figure 5.2 *Senior Executive Development Programme Project plan.*

to facilitate the group work and provide individual coaching on an *ad hoc* basis.

The core aim of Module One was to establish firmly the imperative nature of the corporate challenges and the leaders' responsibilities in addressing them at a personal level. With this group of highly intelligent executives, many of whom were eminent scientists, it was essential to continue the critical dialogue about GW's proposed solution (the SEDP) until they were satisfied that it was a sound approach – they needed to be persuaded by logic. These initial dialogues began to break down the barriers between the participants and initiate relationships between them.

In the three-month break before they met again (at another of the business schools) they received feedback from a 360-degree assessment.

Assessing Leadership Capability

All the information we had gathered during our diagnostic phase was incorporated into an exhaustive tailored evaluation document. The assessment was introduced as part of the development process.

We gathered 360-degree information on each participant from up to 12 senior colleagues, peers and subordinates (and, in some cases, external contacts) about each his or her leadership style. Each was then evaluated against his or her 300 peers.

The Change Partnership handled the feedback reports to maintain confidentiality. Each executive could get his or her feedback from an external or an internal coach. As this was a global group there was a need to work in several languages and to adapt to the national cultural differences. Each quarter, 90 executives needed to meet with a coach who could work in their native language.

When each participant received the 360-degree assessment and feedback his or her coach highlighted up to five developmental issues for him or her to work on in the medium term. The participant was then asked to choose one or two of these which he or she would feel comfortable sharing with a smaller group for discussion and learning in Module Two. The participant and coach then worked together to create a personal development plan.

The assessment process was a massive scheduling and logistical exercise. At each step boundaries were created to protect the integrity of the process and ensure a safe environment for learning. All reports were confidential and held externally by The Change Partnership; and the executive could choose whether or not to make their report open to others.

Module Two

The same groups of executives met again three months after Module One at a different business school.

Having started to form their relationships, and having had time to absorb the learning from Module One and consider themselves in light of their assessments, they were now ready for more intensive personal development. In this second module, the learning sets became much more important forums at which the participants shared their development goals and began to work on them with their peers. This further reinforced the trust between them: personal development work both depends upon and creates trust, making it an essential element of this programme. The participants continued to build partnerships and alliances with each other, making the cross-fertilization of ideas across boundaries and functions possible. Exciting business ideas began to emerge at this stage.

SEDP Summary

Installing a Systematic Process of Key Talent Management

The key talent review process was designed to look holistically at leadership capability. Local businesses would present their key talent on a systematic rolling cycle to the board for review. The process encompassed the following elements:

1. Bench strength analysis (the 360-degree assessment process).

2. Identifying the strategic gaps.

3. Sponsoring development interventions to grow organizational capability through: international assignments; special projects; task forces; virtual team leadership; coaching; competence development; non-executive roles; secondments to external business bodies.

4. Review of key individuals.

5. Review of special groups (women, global/ethnic representation, key functional or technical talent).

6. Using summary reports both as feedback to individuals and as tools for the board to define bench strength and succession issues.

The emphasis was on dialogue, the dynamic use of talent, and remaining in tune with the business as it changed. There was less concern about reporting data and theoretical career planning.

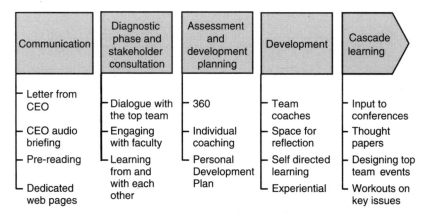

Figure 5.3 *Senior executive development programme summary.*

The Business Deliverables

- By 1999 GW had repaid the borrowings from the acquisition of Wellcome.

- The company had increased the dividend.

- The research and development programme was reinforced and was beginning to deliver new products.

- Restructuring to focus on the customer and improve the development cycle was now taking place.

- Double-digit growth was achieved in 1999.

Success Bred Success

We generated many success stories in the senior executive team. I will give just two examples here.

It was a moment of great achievement when the US team asked the Norwegian general manager to present his 'mega-marketing' ideas to executives in the USA, a recognition that learning from one market could seriously impact and help another to grow revenues.

The Egyptian managing director related how he had tried 11 times to get a product into his portfolio, since he believed it would generate revenue. Each time he had failed to convince the committee that made portfolio decisions, although his business case was compelling. His peer group mentored him and helped him to reframe his proposal. Six weeks later he told his success story to the group. Nine months later he told about the considerable revenue he had generated. When the story was told at a leadership conference, the regional director for Latin America realized the product's potential for his own markets and did a supply deal, generating even more. It was now easier for people to network, to talk about success and failure, to experiment beyond the major markets.

Acknowledging that everyone had development needs had a trans-formational effect on the senior leadership cadre. Suddenly it was acceptable to check out where people had strengths and to locate role models to coach those with developmental needs. This began a process of building trust that extended back into the business. For example: Latin America began globally to leverage licencing agreements, initiating ways of working across boundaries that had previously been untapped. The assessment of executives had huge individual benefit and also brought a new dimension to succession planning and key talent review at an organizational level.

There was growing awareness of the work's significance – academics interested in getting involved in the programme approached me – leading-edge thinkers could see something novel in the making. In 1999 I was invited to make a presentation to the International Consortium for Executive Development Research illus-trating to the business school community how the participant can remain the owner of the learning experience.

The business results continue to speak for themselves.

Any company could deliver such a programme in a scaled-down, but no less effective, form by drawing in people who have expertise in its specific leadership criteria, and using outside consultants for design, quality control and coaching where necessary.

Reaching a Resolution

- What are the strategic drivers for a personal development programme?

- How does our leadership bench strength map against the strategic requirement?

- Am I prepared visibly and actively to support the programme?

- How can I inspire a shift within the top team?

- How would the programme be improved by using external experts?

- Do I need to use multiple institutions in delivery?

- How much time have I got to build my team?

- How long will it take to deliver results through people?

Chapter 6

Managing the Board

Peter Salsbury

Context

An enormous amount of ink has been spent on writing about every aspect of the CEO's role, including the relationship between the CEO and the rest of the board. On the UK side of the Atlantic, the volume of commentary has been vastly expanded since the scandals of the mid-1980s, in particular, the Maxwell case and the various governance committees that resulted.

The issue of CEO and senior executive behaviour was moved to a new level by the spectacular events at Enron which have pushed the pendulum much further towards 'correct governance' than ever. The behaviour of company executives in conjunction with some of the audit partners was clearly unacceptable. However, overreaction will do more harm to the relationship between the CEO and the board – a relationship that already suffers from the pressure of governance on the one hand, and over-exposure of the CEO on the other.

The CEO is now far more visible and, crucially, accountable to a wider spectrum of stakeholders than was the case 15 years ago – which makes it more important than ever that he or she should be able to manage the board. This has been driven by several factors:

● In the UK, Cadbury, through Greenbury and Hampel, highlighted the issues of excess executive power and inadequate shareholder information. They collectively created a new level of disclosure – either through annual reports or the Stock Exchange listing rules.

- There was also a codification of the responsibilities of the entire board, particularly its non-executive – or, more accurately, 'independent' – members. Then accountants, auditors, lawyers (and their attendant consultancy practices) added a plethora of new accounting standards and governance concepts, such as 'risk management', to help the audit committees help the auditors to help the board to show the shareholders that they have satisfied the new strictures of corporate governance!

- Now all non-executives must pass stringent tests of 'independence'. There is a danger that, fearful of accusations of being too close to management, they will be reluctant to get close enough to the executives' running of the company to understand what makes it tick.

All these things add to the CEO's burden: no more cosy, clubby Old Boys' methods; many more administrative minutiae to distract from strategy management; and a nervous, self-protectively distant, non-executive board.

In addition to this, greater pressure on fund managers to meet increasingly ambitious targets has made more prominent the role of financial analysts and sharpened the outside world's focus on CEOs. And then, of course, there is the rapid increase in CEOs' pay generated by the longest and strongest bull market of modern times in the 1990s – nothing is for nothing!

There is one more factor that has changed the role of the CEO, although not a universal one – 'structural isolation'. This came about as corporate structures were flattened during the 1990s, driving out many of the wiser, more experienced, and non-threatening elder statesmen who could give impartial advice because they were not trying to further their own careers.

The combination of non-executive defensiveness and lean executive structures has led to a more isolated breed of CEOs, who have to manage their businesses and their boards with much greater external and internal exposure. Not surprisingly their tenure has become foreshortened, and candidates are asking more questions before accepting these roles.

Managing the board, then, has become just one of a host of new challenges for CEOs. It should not be supposed that it is at the forefront of CEOs' minds on a daily basis. However, they are now much less likely to be also the chairman, and boards (certainly the non-executive parts) are much more likely to be judging their proposals and decisions on the basis of impact on shareholder value than in former years.

A well-run board with the right mix of talents and qualities can be very helpful to the CEO and the company. The virtues of good boards are described in many worthy tracts and particularly biographies. Examples are given of diligence, foresight, wisdom and excellent chairmanship. These 'disciples of Cadbury' have created value by adding to strategy development, supporting the management in tricky times, dealing with succession and ensuring good governance.

On a personal note I shall say that I have been coaching executives professionally for only a year. However, I have been CEO of Marks & Spencer where I saw the workings and behaviours of a board for 10 years. I also sat on the boards of a public utility (NORWEB) and an investment trust (TIRPIT). In the process I experienced both being acquired as well as acquisition. I was able to observe and be part of the complex relationships and motivations that influence board decision on strategic direction or succession.

I have had the privilege of conversations with, and advice from, many extremely experienced business leaders, particularly during periods of enormous pressure as CEO at M&S. Those two years were an intense learning experience as well as a time of difficulty. The learning was greatly assisted by a very experienced coach, who helped me work out my own way forward by a combination of questions and challenges which expanded my breadth of consideration, bringing aspects of life ambitions as well as business needs into balance when making decisions.

Cause and effect is imperfect, and the behaviour and motivations of people are no more predictable in the boardroom than in any other walk of life. (I often think that a large family is a good parallel.) The CEO is continually playing percentage shots when making decisions. Difficult and controversial decisions face him or her every day and often the sheer pace of change makes considered decision making all-but impossible. The CEO must learn to live with the consequences of his or her decisions, good or bad. Learning to accept ambiguity and imperfection is an essential skill for every CEO.

I will not attempt to add to the virtuous examples of excellence I referred to earlier. Instead, I will look at the less perfect reality of a new CEO who has the day-to-day pressures of delivering short-term performance numbers while dealing with a board, some of whose members have their own agendas as well the company's. A coach is like a friend to a client: he or she can challenge, caution, guide and advise, but can't make the client listen. The CEO in this scenario, partially due to 'selective hearing', and partially because he was overwhelmed by the pace at which his situation was changing, failed to listen – with predictable results.

I hope you will find some practical tips on avoiding pitfalls – or at least some clues as to where you might find a rope ladder to help you scramble out of any pit into which you might stray.

The scenario is based on my own experience of management as a CEO, a coach and a client.

Client Company Profile

Henry Grafton plc (HG) – UK is an importer of toys and games, and manufacturer/marketer of toiletries and homoeopathic medicines. A family toy business founded in 1935, HG grew steadily under Henry and his son Thomas. It was floated in 1984. In 1992, Thomas bought a small homoeopathic medicine company that flourished, as did the toiletries business, but toys were static and profits fell for four years before stabilizing at a disappointing level. When Thomas died suddenly in 1996 the family owned 25% of the business.

A new non-executive chairman was appointed, and the director of toys became the company's first CEO. He took a cautious approach, and profits were maintained at a satisfactory level through cost control rather than expansion. He suddenly retired in 1999 and, on his recommendation, the marketing director was appointed to replace him.

The figures: 2000/01 – turnover £280 million (£250 million previous year); profits before tax £19 million (£21 million previous year).

The Client

Steven Frost, 42, married with two sons aged 15 and 12. After eight years at Unilever and two at Andersen Consulting, he was recruited as a director by Thomas Grafton. He impressed the board as a successful leader of sales and marketing but, to be frank, the internal competition wasn't impressive. He had now been a board member for four years and group sales and marketing director for two. His reputation was as a demanding, but supportive leader with good commercial judgement based on understanding the market. Full of ideas, he worked hard at his external network, bringing deals through for his division in the face of stiff competition. His appointment as CEO was not unanimous: the selectors felt he might lack the focus and determination to lead the board as a former colleague, and that he was handicapped by his lack of hands-on experience in the toy business.

The Challenge

Three months after his appointment, HG's performance was poor and Steven had had a tough time at recent board meetings. In his new position, he was failing to convey the enthusiasm and confidence with which he had inspired his team as marketing director, and his handling of board meetings was failing to impress. He faced four clear challenges at this point:

- His preparation for the CEO role had been inadequate in relation to the non-executive board.

- The demands of board matters were taking up too much time.

- He had to find a way of dealing with the under-performing toys division.

- He must give more priority to managing board meetings and his primary role at them.

The Desired Results

- To take charge by asserting himself with the board.

- To improve his networking among the non-executives.

- To gain credibility with the board by (a) developing relationships with its members and (b) reviving the toys division.

- To develop and implement a growth strategy.

The Developing Approach

Steven was 'sent' to me by his chairman (Sir Anthony Piper) and company secretary/HR Director (Owen Graham) because he needed help from a coach with CEO experience. They had reassured Steven of their confidence in him, their intervention made him feel threatened and patronized so when we met for our initial 'chemistry meeting' he was cool. It soon became clear that he didn't know that reservations had been expressed about him at his appointment, although I did.

I told Steven that, while Tony and Owen might suggest specific areas for improvement, my role was to work through his own require-ments – and to begin by helping him clarify them. The temperature rose and we agreed to start with a half-day session, at which we would assess his requirements in the context of his life in and out of Grafton, and establish what he had done with his time during the three months since his appointment.

Though he was limiting the time dedicated to the media, Steven was spending a great deal of time networking with senior board members' business friends (all much older and, in his view, mainly past it or irrelevant), and fulfilling engagements bequeathed by his predecessor. We agreed that he would come to the next meeting armed with a log of his activities and his thoughts on agenda priorities. He was naturally keen to address the issue of the board and agreed to give me a summary before our next meeting.

We started our next session by looking at how his working time compared with his priorities, which were primarily operational and specifically revolved around the toys business. (A costly sick man since it accounted for more than half the company's total turnover.)

His analysis revealed that he was spending much more time on board-related matters than he had thought. In the past four weeks, as well as the monthly board meeting he had spent time on:

- An audit committee meeting.
- The risk management map for the audit committee.
- Weekly meetings with the chairman.
- Briefings from the communications department.
- HR and remuneration policy discussions.

Too many of these were group meetings, at which there would be no opportunity to build individual relationships. I suggested that Steven should build one-to-one time with his executive board members into his agenda by, for instance: arranging short weekly meetings with the finance and HR directors.

Meetings with his operational reports were taking longer than he thought they should, because he was still getting to know their areas, and he had left the two executives who were running his old area pretty much alone.

We put this to one side and worked through analysing what he wanted to achieve both in work and outside. When we discussed his style of leadership, he claimed to be a collaborative boss who liked to lead by example. He spent time listening to his people and encouraging them. When asked how he dealt with conflict and other difficult situations, like poor performance, he said that he was always prepared to research, arrive at and deliver a decision face-to-face. (Sadly, the above traits were not in evidence in his later dealings with the board.)

We then talked through his vision for HG. Steven saw the company's future as supplying beauty and well-being products to major retail chains. There were three points of competitive advantage: an integrated product offer, including own label; a low cost base; and a full merchandizing and distribution system. He became really enthusiastic describing how this would build and eventually develop an international capability. The plan required acquisition and disposal, most notably of the Toys business, which led us back to the current issues of handling the board.

Stephen's Analysis of the Board

The board meets monthly on a Thursday morning followed by lunch.

Non-executive board:

- Chairman: Sir Anthony Piper. Accountant. Top-five partnership. Knighted for his work as head of the audit commission. A founder member of the board, appointed on the recommendation of the investment bank who handled the flotation. Became chairman four years ago. Uses his position to support his many committee memberships and *pro-bono* directorships. He's a supporter of mine, but pompous and patronizing.

- Richard Rafter. Engineer and retired former CEO of a machine tool company. Recruited by Tony Piper as the 'production, and quality expert' and chair of audit committee. Dour but straight. Takes the business very seriously. Has very firm views on board process and governance.

- Piers Alcock. Marketing executive with Unilever brand experience. Brought onto the board by Thomas G, largely for his experience in the branded soaps business. Runs own business. Chair of remuneration and nomination committees. Worthy, but no real track record of achievement. Likes you to think he's known by the great and the good.

● Harry Grafton. Grandson of the founder. Thorn in my side. Worked for HG as a young man but didn't like life in Daddy's shadow. Left and set up own business. Now he's the senior Grafton he's become the defender of the 'spirit' of the business, which entails a vociferous reactionary stance.

● Peter Burston. Marketing director of a clothing retail plc. Recommended to Tony Piper by his Chairman, who sees a bright future and recommended him. Enthusiastic and quick to acquaint himself with the business and its key players. My own age and the only non-exec who's a real ally.

Executive board:

● Simon Liptrott. Finance director. Chartered accountant. Rigorous. Punctilious. Guards 'his' numbers jealously and tells his team to do likewise, so we have a plethora of independent systems devised at local level instead of good management accounts. Reasonable external relations with investors. Seen as (and is!) sound but unexciting. Chair of audit committee.

● Peter Swann. Senior of the two chemists who founded the homoeopathic medicine business bought by HG in 1992. Not a great corporate contributor but expert in his field, which operates independently from the rest of the business and with some success. I like him.

● Edward Roberts. Toys director. Promoted by the former CEO at the same time as I was made director of sales and marketing. Many years' experience in Toys. Takes a more hands-off approach than the directors of the other divisions. Some resentment towards me – thought he should have been a candidate for the CEO role. I don't rate him, or trust him.

● Owen Graham. Company secretary and HR director. Lawyer with Audit Commission experience. Brought in as company secretary with brief to modernize governance systems. Appointed to the board when he took over Personnel (now HR) role. Has flair and a sense of humour.

● There is no sales and marketing director, so that division's two senior executives report directly to me.

We started by going through the non-executives one by one, and it became apparent that Steven had little rapport with them, apart from Peter Burston who was roughly his own age. Even the chairman seemed a bit distant. The executive board was a different matter, but not without issues. Steven saw Peter Swann, who headed the homoeopathic business, as a star, thanks to his enormous input in developing Steven's ideas for the future. Thanks to their shared sense of humour Owen Graham was becoming an ally, with great potential in a growing business. Interestingly, Steven didn't see HR as Owen's strength. His problems were a difficult relationship with Edward Roberts, the toys director, and a finance director who was competent, but whose secretive management style would not serve the company's aspirations. On the plus side, there were at least three non-board executives who had the capability to go much further.

In preparing for our meeting Steven had considered his readiness for the role of CEO. He had concluded that much more time should have been spent getting to know his colleagues, particularly the non-execs, whom he had hardly seen apart from at board meetings and occasional dinners. We agreed that he would meet each board member individually to establish rapport.

He had been aware of all the issues among his executive colleagues well before his appointment but had not raised them, and had not been invited to. He had now developed a very substantial agenda that he needed to address, which would transform the company but he didn't feel that he had the support to drive it through.

Steven now told me that he was going to intervene operationally in the toys division. He didn't believe that the right steps had been taken yet, despite having said that they had at the last board meeting.

We agreed that we would come back to this, but that his most immediate problem revolved around board meetings and his main role at them. I decided that a rather more directive approach would be acceptable. It was Tony Piper's style to ask each executive director to describe his monthly performance and issues, with Steven invited to summarize at the end. This had been the pattern under Steven's predecessor, who had been quite laid back. The arrival of Richard Rafter and Peter Burston had introduced a more challenging tone, and the deterioration of performance had put pressure on the executives, and Steven in particular. Operational intervention from the top was essential at this point, but Steven had no CEO experience of his own to help him formulate a strategy, and his relationships with other board members were not such that he felt he could ask their advice without looking weak.

I suggested that he should see the chairman, Tony Piper, urgently and tell him that, in future, he would lead the monthly reporting section of the meeting himself, calling on his colleagues to contribute as required. This reversal would focus the discussions more closely on the CEO's priorities, and demonstrate clearly that Steven was in control. Steven liked the suggestion and said he would also warn Tony that he was going to insist on change in the Toys operation.

After that meeting, Steven told me that Tony had been pleased with his initiative and endorsed his approach to board meetings. Several pieces of information, which Tony gave him during the meeting, had made Steven decide not to go through the strategic plans with Tony, and to pause before continuing his round of one-to-ones with the non-execs.

Firstly, Tony told Steven that Richard Rafter had reservations about his appointment as CEO and was still not convinced. Rafter was unhappy about the standard of some areas of governance; the flimsy risk management and lack of executive board involvement; the quality of reports from the internal auditor; and the share option scheme that was not performance related. He also felt that the finance director had taken far too long to inform the board of a pension fund deficit and his plans to remedy it, and questioned Harry Grafton's independence as a non-executive director.

Tony saw these points as criticism of himself as well as other members of the board, but was particularly hurt by the suggestion that Henry Grafton was not independent, as it undermined his own judgement. He suggested that Steven respond positively to Richard Rafter as soon as possible. Steven was surprised at the weakness of this response, although he accepted that there was some substance behind the criticisms. Given the fact that Richard Rafter had little confidence in him as CEO, Steven needed to work out the best response.

When we met the following day Steven delivered two further pieces of bad news: the half year figures would almost certainly be accompanied by a profits warning; and there was going to be a major product recall of a soft toy the next day, caused by a safety problem.

Steven was aware of the danger of being overwhelmed by the whirlwind of events. I told him that he needed to stop, look and re-prioritize, so we started by listing the issues.

We had already identified the board problems, preparing as the CEO, and taking control when getting started. Now the operational issue was going to become mixed with these issues as lower profits led to investor questions and disappointment. In addition Steven was faced with a chairman who felt challenged by Richard Rafter, a zealous board member who was using governance issues to make his point and, perhaps, to further his own ambitions.

I warned Steven that he was now in danger of being embroiled in, and waylaid by, board dissonance. Obviously the profits warning was now the immediate priority – but I insisted that we should take some time to work out how he could manage the board problem. After all, I pointed out, without the board's support he would be impotent and potentially redundant.

How bad would the profits warning be and could the analysis accompanying the story help to lesson the negative impact? The single most important factor in calming the financial stakeholders would be to come up with a strategic plan for improving the toys division's under-performance, which had been brought to the fore by the product recall. Our discussions resulted in the following plan:

- Position the toys business for sale in the medium-term by moving his sales manager and a small team into the business with a remit to dramatically improve sales in the short term.

- Get rid of the toys director, Ed Roberts, either through the sale or redundancy in the medium term.

- Use Ed's board vacancy to promote the sales manager, thereby gaining a friend on the board!

Steven was using a PR company to help frame the financial announcement, had taken advice from an investment bank, and was now confident that the changes he would impose on the toys business would restore short-term profitability. Could he buy some time with the financial analysts? How would the board react, especially Richard Rafter, whose instinct would probably be to insist on an immediate release of the profits warning as required by the Stock Exchange?

Steven talked me through these issues very calmly, and with more authority than he had shown before. Why was this? He said he was always energized by a crisis and became very calm. Secondly, he now felt in command operationally and was genuinely confident that the numbers would come round in a few months.

Perhaps the problem could be used to achieve some progress on Steven's objectives? We decided that he would take advantage of the crisis to establish a rapport with and respect from the board by quickly demonstrating his control. When we parted he had decided to see or telephone every director and recommend that, as the mid-term prospects would be quite stable, there was no need for an early profits warning. He would present his proposed Stock Exchange statements for the press conference at the next board meeting, the day before the interim results.

Steven and I shaped his statement, which said, first and foremost, that a quality assurance team would be going in to the toys division to ensure the highest standards of safety. He added that a dedicated sales team was already in place to revitalize the division's sales, and money was being invested to ensure its success. The sales team was expected to improve results dramatically within the next quarter.

He finished by saying that, although profits were lower than expected, they remained within the realm of other competitors'.

The statement was delivered and the numbers announced:

- It was seen as only a moderate profits warning (in the context of similar companies). The share price dropped 20% then came back by 10%.

- The product recall had been bungled and caused some sarcastic press comment.

- Steven had supportive messages from Owen Graham on behalf of the executives plus Peter Burston (his closest non-exec colleague) and, surprisingly to Steven, Richard Rafter.

He telephoned me with the news and I congratulated him on a disaster averted.

At our next meeting we summarized the situation regarding the board, looking at progress or the lack of it:

- Three of his four executive directors, especially Owen Graham, were very much with him, but Ed Roberts had become distinctly nervous as he felt undermined by Steven's instruction.

- The chairman seemed to have withdrawn, and Harry Grafton and Piers Alcock were not interested in dialogue with Steven. On the plus side, Steven's fire-fighting had built a bridge with Richard Rafter and a bond was growing with Peter Burston.

- The operational improvements were work in progress.

- Several months had passed and Steven's long-term strategy had not even been discussed.

I was horrified by Steven's isolation on the non-executive board, particularly his impasse with Anthony Piper. Without the support of his chairman the whole company could stall. I urged him to learn the reason for the coolness between them.

Caught in the maelstrom, Steven had failed to take sufficient notice of my repeated advice to build relationships with the board. He had not *heard* me say that, based on my own experience, I *knew* this was almost the most important thing he could do. He felt that he 'didn't have time' to do it. Big mistake! The recent emergency had led him to act alone, without collaborating with the board or seeking its members' wisdom. He had imposed his will, communicated mainly by telephone and, in general, risked such fragile alliances as had existed. His behaviour had been understandable in a crisis – and had certainly shown him to be in control. It would have been accepted had he developed relationships with his colleagues in advance. As it stood, most of them were alienated if not frankly furious.

A fresh attempt at bridge building was essential. We agreed that he would improve the situation by the following means:

● Spending time with individual board members, formally and informally, to build trust.

● Consulting them, individually and collectively, on planning the company's strategy.

● Drawing out their individual views on difficult issues to retain a realistic view of the board's temperature.

Steven then took a previously booked three-week break, and we did not meet again for six weeks.

During the break, Steven had given further consideration to his long-term strategy of moving the company more firmly into health and beauty supply, and had begun work on an acquisition proposition. A cosmetics company had been introduced as a prospect by an investment bank. He had arranged an offsite meeting with the non-executive board for the following week. At this meeting he proposed to present his grand plan, including the disposal of toys as well as the cosmetics company purchase. Once again, no board members had been consulted in advance.

The toy business had just about stabilized, but he was having real problems with Ed Roberts who resented Steven's 'interference' in his area. The bankers had told Steven that Ed was a handicap to selling the business and must be moved elsewhere. Steven did not want Ed in the firm much longer – for him, part of the benefit of selling the Toy business would be getting rid of Ed with it! In short – Ed Roberts would have to go. Steven would then promote his sales manager into the vacant sales and marketing position on the board once the toys business was sold.

It was good to see Steven so fired up, but we needed to talk this through carefully. He did not have the support he needed for his strategy, and had no real knowledge of where some of the non-execs were coming from. Now he needed to fire one of his executive colleagues as well. It was clear to me that the discussions we had had before his holidays had been utterly ignored and Steven had not built any relationships or gained the input of any board member apart from Peter Swann while developing his strategy.

The plan seemed a good one, but it couldn't go any further without involving the FD, Simon Liptrott, who was a danger because he was so cautious he would probably run straight to the Chairman to cover his back. We talked through various options and Steven eventually realized that he would simply have to intimidate Simon into silence. He was going to tell Simon that Richard Rafter – of whom Simon was afraid – had asked Steven to assess the value of the toys business without either the chairman or Harry Grafton knowing.

Steven had also thought that getting rid of Ed Roberts would be difficult unless he could find a way of making his incompetence obvious. Ed was very much part of the firm and had a good rapport with Harry Grafton, who was probably an opponent of the toys business sale. Was this the right route? After all nothing had changed and Ed was no worse now than he had been for years. By contrast with his sneaky approach with Simon, Steven decided that in Ed's case he would tell all the board (except Harry Grafton and, of course, Ed himself) the truth about the bankers' view of Ed.

Steven asked if he could touch base if necessary in between the stages of implementing his plot and then he left.

As it turned out, it was Owen Graham who phoned me first. Owen had been Steven's first port of call and he was worried that Steven's tactics might backfire. However, he also said that there had been an obvious improvement in Steven's confidence, which both Tony Piper and Richard Rafter had mentioned to him. I thought this might be a useful boost for Steven so I called him to pass the information on. He told me that both Peter Burston and Richard Rafter had advised him not to pussyfoot around with Ed. He was CEO, and if he needed Ed out to achieve his strategy then he must get on with it. But he must keep the board informed.

I learned what happened next from the press, in a short piece saying that there was to be a trade sale of the H Grafton toys business and that Ed Roberts had resigned to pursue other interests. No mention of cosmetics as yet. Steven and I met again later that week. He was quite tired and not as chirpy as I had expected.

He was, of course, pleased that his disposal plan had been adopted, but his lack of knowledge of the board had produced a surprise. Harry Grafton had found out about the cosmetics plan – almost certainly from the FD, Simon Liptrott – and lobbied both the chairman and Piers Alcock against it.

Steven also learned that the banker he was using on the purchase had fallen out with Tony, the chairman, during his time at the Audit Commission, which explained his recent *froideur*. The cosmetics acquisition was on hold. As Tony seemed to take these things personally, there was no way Steven could proceed without an effective ally in charge of the mergers and acquisitions, someone who had the chairman's confidence.

The share price had recovered to just about where it was before the profits warning.

We had reached a watershed. Our work is still in progress, but Steven learned a great deal and made significant progress over the year. He asserted himself with the board during the crisis and averted disaster with the press and the financial community. He developed and implemented a toys division strategy, which revived it in the short term and shuffled it off in the long. *But!* He had still failed to improve his relationships with most board members, or, indeed, to build them. This had stopped him from implementing his cosmetics strategy. This fundamental issue will be the prime focus of our ongoing work.

Reaching a Resolution

To handle the board you need to consider the following questions:

- What are the board's strengths, weaknesses and other interests?
- Is the chairman strong and supportive of you?
- Were you a unanimous choice? If not, who was against you and why?
- How is the board run, and does it give a satisfactory picture of board behaviour?
- Is board governance at an acceptable level?
- Who stands where on the key issues?
- Are you seen to be confident and in charge, especially at set pieces?
- Are there any people issues to deal with? If so, how will you manage them?
- Have you made a positive impression on all the key players?
- How are you going to get your strategic priorities agreed and supported?

Now this is one VATman I'm pleased to see.

Chapter 7

Communicating with all of the Stakeholders all of the Time

Robin Linnecar

Context

Sadly, what you say and what comes across are often two totally different things. Who is addressed and who ought to be addressed also often turn out to be different. Communication, one of the CEO's most sophisticated tools, must be used with precision and care. If it is not, things may quickly go awry.

A CEO had been asked by the chairman to present the annual results at the AGM. He intended to say that great progress had been made over the year and the company was now on an even keel after a difficult time. He began by saying: 'Last year our business was standing on the edge of an abyss. This year, I am delighted to say, we have taken a giant leap forward!' An old chestnut, but there is no better demonstration of the importance of clarity and planning in communication to stakeholders!

Conveying what you mean to say demands continual thought and organization, especially in times of change. It is easy to get it wrong and, in doing so, to make a difficult situation worse. Be it strong, weak, mixed, wrong, non-committal or non-existent, a message can make or mar the situation. And the absence of a timely message may do the same. Communication matters!

The CEO of any public company is responsible for communicating appropriately and effectively with a long and diverse list of stakeholders, including:

● The non-executive directors.

● The executive board or committee.

● The banks.

● Investment fund managers.

● Analysts.

● Auditors.

● Lawyers.

● Employees.

● The media.

● Customers.

● Suppliers.

The purpose of any communication varies with the audience. For example, in the list above, the board will wish to be able to discuss strategic matters, and expect the CEO to be comfortable in both setting out the vision and being challenged. Analysts, brokers and other report writers will expect consistency over time, and candid statements about the state of the business. Employees will expect to be regarded by the CEO as a collection of individuals. Ultimately, all messages to these parties must be consistent.

An apposite example is to be found in the following case.

The board of a company in the entertainment games industry approved a proposal to seek a purchaser. The company had three particularly strong products, but lacked the distributive muscle to make real headway in markets outside the UK. Without access to such markets it could not succeed in the longer term. A trade sale was seen as the likeliest outcome.

The decision to sell had to be kept secret – for practical and Stock Exchange reasons – so the CEO established a near-continuous dialogue with the FD, Chairman and senior non-exec director about strategy and tactics. They gathered the necessary material for the corporate finance deal-makers to be able to move as quickly as possible from offer for sale, through enquirers in a data room, to heads of agreement and then exclusivity with an identified buyer. The CEO also used executive meetings to reassure his directors that this strategy was sound. It was not an easy communication. The remaining executive directors knew the CEO would not retain a leadership role (maybe any role) after the sale – and so could sell his shares and move on, while they, perhaps, remained to work out the future with a new owner.

Almost inevitably, the press got wind of something happening in the industry. Speculation grew. Newspapers began to postulate likely 'marriages' between companies. The CEO began to spend a lot of time on the road, talking to analysts and financial, PR and corporate finance advisers to ensure a consistent message which did not dissemble, gave away no unnecessary information, and kept accord with previously published company reports. These discussions were vital since share price stability had to be maintained while discussions proceeded.

While all this was going on, the employees remained in ignorance of any impending deal, which created another delicate communications need.

The first opportunity to talk to employees came only when the sale had been agreed and a date fixed to 'go public'. At that point, the CEO had to communicate clearly and boldly that the new owner represented the best way forward for the company. Employee concerns were focused on the implications for jobs, location and culture. The CEO would need to use every channel at his disposal – as well as putting together a very convincing case.

In the event, the CEO successfully cleared all these communications hurdles, and the sale went through almost without a hitch. The case illustrates how the common range and complexity of communications demands adds hugely to the CEO's workload and pressures at times of crisis or change. Keeping all communications activities under control, on time, and on message can remind a harassed CEO of a plate-spinning act – just when it seems the last plate is spinning, wobbles appear elsewhere in the line!

As a prerequisite, any CEO needs to understand his or her audience, and be able to talk to that audience with conviction, but the problem usually is that the CEO does not have the luxury of an extended timetable and so is too busy to set time aside to communicate well. This creates a communications 'Molotov cocktail' which can wreck a career. Figure 7.1 helps to explain this.

Of course this exaggerates somewhat to make a point, and a 'delivery focus' can lead to healthy communication. More commonly it does not. In an environment of clear vision, common values, good management and good leadership the quality rather than the quantity of communication is what matters. Very often, however, the circle shown above applies – an over-emphasis on 'task' means people find little time or inclination to communicate. This may be

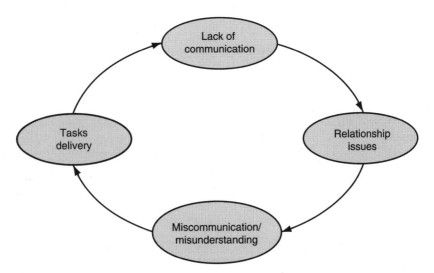

Figure 7.1 *Consequences for a frenetic organization.*

compounded by a reward system which encourages people to get on and 'do' – even if only to protect their bonuses. In turn, working relationships have no time to develop. The result is miscommunication or misunderstanding, because good communication cannot be just 'switched on'. It has to be practised to become perfect. If it is not, it goes wrong, because the communicator does not know the audience well enough, or because that audience has no reason to trust the message. Functional silo management, a lack of cross-selling of ideas/views and of staff transfers between divisions may be the resultant corporate behaviours.

Client Company Profile

Op Co is in the utilities business. It is European-based, operating in the UK. The CEO in this scenario is head of the UK organization (responsible for all UK and Continental operations). A consortium holding company (Consortium Hold Co) representing three countries – UK, France and the Netherlands – sets the overall strategy. Each country has a company that is an equal shareholder in the consortium. UK Co is a private organization, while the French (Nat Fran) and Dutch (Nat Hol) companies are nationalized.

All three shareholders in the Consortium have separate businesses in their home countries which operate globally, and this utilities 'venture' run for them by Op Co represents less than 5% of their turnover in each business. The Consortium board meets eight times a year with James, as Op Co CEO, always present. Chairmanship of the board rotates between the three countries on a six-monthly basis.

The Client

James is 50 years old, seasoned and experienced in the utilities sector, mainly in electricity but also in water. He has been involved with unionized labour in the UK, has been in operational, marketing and customer service roles and was, until recently, in charge of project managing the design, building and acceptance of major new infrastructure in the UK. In the three years prior to taking up the CEO role at Op Co, he was director of operations in his previous company. When I began to coach him he had been in this, his first, CEO role for only six months.

The Challenge

The challenge facing James was formidable and many-faceted, and he felt very isolated in the new CEO role.

The previous finance director had recently quit, so James had a major vacancy in his team. This was critical, as he needed to produce the annual budget for the board within two months. A new FD was swiftly appointed but then two other directors resigned, leaving him with a young and relatively inexperienced team of four. He now needed to get the right people in place and to develop his team as an imperative.

Compounding all this were the conflicting agendas of the consortium members. Since UK Co was a private company, it took a short-term, cash-oriented approach. Nat Fran followed a much longer-term strategy, and Nat Hol took the middle road. Both European companies wanted to be 'visible' in the UK in order to win further opportunities elsewhere in the world, and this mattered more than Op Co's immediate results.

Board meetings of the holding company were very formal. Because of vested interests, there were few opportunities for discussion, and meetings were designed to produce carefully monitored minutes, according to a standing agenda. The hard work and influencing were to be done outside these meetings. James faced the following board issues:

- Given the mixed board agendas, what exactly did he need to communicate?

- Who needed to know what and when?

- Who had most influence on whom? And what could be fed in through a 'friendly' member?

- Which discussions could be kept confidential?

- James then discovered (through industry contacts) that UK Co, and especially the new finance director, wanted to replace him as CEO. They wanted to put in their own person as CEO. Evidence such covert antagonism left James was despondent and tempted to 'throw in the towel'.

Desired Results

- To craft appropriate and mutually non-conflicting messages for all stakeholders, and to communicate them.

- To raise James's awareness of the disparate political and business agendas of the Consortium members.

- To bring the members together through a programme of targeted communication.

- To help James inspire his team to deliver operational results.

- To help James free up his time for planning and delivering effective communications.

- To support James in developing ways to build good relationships in a hostile situation.

- To give James someone to talk to in a confidential environment and to plan a strategy of whom to talk to in developing a career 'Plan B' – what to do if things fall apart.

The Developing Approach

James was married, with children, and set great store by traditional family values and activities – things like taking holidays together, eating meals together and talking together. He described himself to me as fair, encouraging, supportive and clear in his relationship with his children. In the course of this, he volunteered an additional piece of self-knowledge: 'my nature is to try and conform and not stand out from the crowd.' These approaches and attitudes were carried over into his working life and were embellished with his key attribute: a democratic, open, consultative style. All this was to prove immensely helpful in his relationships with the consortium members.

Although previously in a related industry in the same sector, he now found the isolated role of CEO difficult. Because of his new position, people around him communicated with him and treated him differently. This was affecting his normal style of communication. The way the consortium members behaved also made life more difficult for James. For example, the chairman of the consortium did not expect James to give anyone 'bad news'. Any shortfalls in revenues and overruns on costs had to be expressed sensitively, and the chairman always had to be the first to know. The UK Co member, on the other hand, was keen to push James hard to take costs out and deliver improved results – and he was not above doing this in a bullying way. The politically astute Nat Hol member was open with James in expressing a desire to buy up some of UK Co's shareholding, which, of course, raised other issues. Only the Nat Fran member seemed to be neutral.

At our first coaching meetings we established how James had approached events and activities in his life to date, and in particular what forms and styles of communication he had used. Though this was the first time James had held a CEO position, it was important for him to recognize that his previous style of communication could work well in his new position. In addition, I had James identify people and concepts he had admired in his past – what we christened his 'admirations'. We talked about his previous bosses over the years, as well as individuals and situations he had come across in business. As we did so, we discovered key qualities in the leaders which he found admirable, and with which he identified – things such as:

- Setting clear expectations of what was wanted, when it was wanted – and the consequences of non-delivery.

- An intuitive ability to mix business with pleasure, and to make work fun.

- 'He gave me a sense of strategy, and the vision, the big picture.'

- 'He could engage people in what he was feeling, while still being thorough, accurate and able to marshal just the right argument for the moment.'

- Being very open and flexible with tactics to achieve the key strategic objectives.

Some simple solutions came to mind. For example, we agreed that he would make better use of the not infrequent travel time with the UK Co representatives before meetings. James was to set himself specific objectives for each 'meeting' while travelling together. James identified which issues he could air, and to what extent he would commit himself to prospective targets. A bonus of doing this would be that it would give him and his team something to communicate to Op Co generally, and something at which to aim. A prime learning point for James in this was that while he was keenly aware of his own agenda and all the problems he had to solve, he had spent little time thinking about others' agendas. If he could help other consortium members achieve their individual objectives it might open up all sorts of possibilities for mutual help. But to realize this, he had to free up time to be able to communicate in ways which were appropriate to each consortium member.

After our fourth meeting, a new appointment meant that James would have to communicate with a totally new individual. UK Co appointed a new finance director, who put its investment under intense scrutiny. Word came through in various 'urgent' meetings with James and his own Finance team that costs had to be taken out of Op Co's business at a faster and more extreme rate than before. It was deemed necessary in UK Co's eyes to appoint someone alongside James to go through the books and analyse where costs could be cut, because it had not been done well enough to date. The message as received by James not only was that his job was on the line, but also that there was another person whose introduction further complicated matters. James knew this person was being slated to take over as CEO – which was all the more galling since the previous UK Co representative had reported back to the

UK Co board that the results were coming good! The new FD wanted to look good by delivering rapid and relentless cost cutting – which, in James's view, could jeopardize the improvement in performance.

In his frustration and anger at being treated in this way when results were good, James was tempted to resign but, despite his pique, he knew that this was not the best solution. All was not lost. James needed to be reminded that Nat Fran and Nat Hol were supporters of his, as was the consortium's chairman. The shareholdings were unlikely to change, and his position was secure providing Nat Fran and Nat Hol supported him. Thus it was imperative that he keep in close communication with the French and Dutch, to ensure their needs were being met so that their support was assured. James talked to his chairman and won an assurance that the various members were aware of what UK Co was attempting, and that Nat Fran and Nat Hol would not support any attempt to oust James. Keeping this support was crucial. We discussed how James could keep his composure at forthcoming meetings and communicate his successful control of the business.

Eight months after appointment, James' own contract was still to be formalized and, obviously, this came high on his list of communication topics – he had to find support from the consortium members in securing his contract. We developed a strategy of relationship building by telephone, confrontation, face-to-face meeting, the written word and presentation. The outline of this was developed in the face-to-face session in my office with an analysis of the various options and tactics available to James.

One aim of the short-term strategy was to resist the imposition of an outsider to review costs. The criteria for this resistance, and how these would be communicated, were defined to James's satisfaction. Drawing on the way he had tackled some matters in the past was crucial to James' success. He had begun by being more concerned with his 'dented pride' and 'outrage'. Learning to manage his emotion, in order to manage the situation better, was key to success, as James soon concluded, in our joint explorations.

Time was at a premium. James had to seize every opportunity to communicate with key people in his world travel with consortium members whenever possible. This would give him a captive audience! He carefully worked up an agenda for each such encounter, which included communicating information on the state of the business, on what was planned, on what had been set in motion, and on what had been achieved.

James also created further effective communicating time by ensuring that he had a significant influence on the agendas of all meetings. He found he was able to augment the standing agenda of the normal Consortium board meetings. This was achieved mostly by judiciously telephoning the chairman and alerting him to the issues which really needed to be resolved. James did this knowing full well that the chairman would see the need to advise and consult other Consortium board members, in this way doing some of James' communicating and influencing work for him!

At the same time James was at pains to keep his team fully informed of directions and plans in the business, by involving them in drawing up a new budget for the new UK Co FD. Without immersing them in all of the politics of the situation, James was able to engage his own team and get their full commitment.

This helped to ward off the appointment of the proposed UK Co watchdog. It also enabled James to free up more of his own time to concentrate on the politics and relationships around him. To help build an atmosphere of trust among his key team members, he organized 'offsite' meetings, lasting for up to a couple of days, in order to be able to work through the more difficult issues. On each occasion, James worked hard to ensure he was unfailingly clear and decisive in communicating his intentions. None of this deterred James from frequent visits to the various locations in the UK and the Continent, to provide necessary 'moral support' to local managers, and to be seen and heard articulating and reinforcing the Op Co strategy. He also used video communication to send regular messages to staff.

In our sessions together we also spent a long time talking about the key ingredients of good delegation, to enable his directors, managers and staff to take some of the load off him by ensuring issues were dealt with at the lowest possible level of accountability. It also served to cement the team, and to accelerate the development of its members.

James' natural way of working tended to be more consultative than authoritarian, and there were some situations with his directors in which he was tempted to stick with this natural style when, in fact, a more authoritarian style was necessary. For a while this was a handicap, but, gradually, he became aware of the need for flexible, situational leadership, the style and context of communication of whose communication were dictated by circumstance rather than personality.

To demonstrate the need for flexibility, I shared with James the example of a telecommunications CEO whose authoritarian style created problems. When his first major crisis arose, he decided to engage in direct personal e-mail communication with all staff, to show that he was leading effectively. The tone of the e-mails was personal, direct from the CEO and, unsurprisingly, it conveyed more accurately his own personal view than that of a united top team. This exacerbated an already tense situation. In particular, he alienated many key managers, who legitimately felt that it was part of their role to communicate to their own people. They felt that he had usurped their role, and damaged their credibility. Unscrambling the damaged morale and relationships took much time and effort. The lesson is that, before you take action which bypasses the accepted hierarchy and systems, you must first consult and involve other key players. The best of intentions can backfire unless everyone who should be involved is involved.

James attended regular monthly board meetings with the holding companies, and soon learned that it was better to use time outside the meetings to influence and persuade, than to be contentious within them. We worked on several dynamics to help him in this:

- Looking at the other person's agenda, and targeting communication at it to enable a 'win/win' situation. This worked especially well around the personal agendas of the respective consortium members, as these related to James and Op Co.

- Using 'scenario building' to depict different (but always plausible) futures so that communication for most eventualities could be considered in advance. This helped particularly when thinking through potential changes in shareholding amongst the consortium members, and what fresh dynamics would result from them. The other important area related to political decisions impacting the industry which might be made by the UK, the Netherlands and France.

- Reviewing James' style of thinking to allow for different communication in meetings. This was particularly helpful as some board members thought financially, some tactically/politically, some strategically – and some only about their own reputations! Fathoming the mindset and thinking pattern in each case enabled him to develop different styles to complement his own naturally analytical and financial approach.

- We explored the difference between assertion, persuasion, aggression and 'bridging' styles of influencing. In spite of this, it was almost inevitable, given the different relationships with his board, team of directors, staff and colleagues, that situations arose which tempted the involvement of the media. Thus one more set of stakeholders was added to James' list. The external relationships with customers and the media would become a key ingredient in his work.

Several incidents early in his tenure attracted press coverage, and James and his PR director were called upon to make comment. health and safety provided the first main area of media interest and attention. The fact that the company had employees in several different countries meant that not only did employee relations take on more of an international flavour (with all the attendant complications), but also that the reporting structure had new political significance. While James was in charge of the consortium's operations, and thus of all the employees, he had to be very clear about the respective members' national political interests. Thus he had to be sure to present events in as favourable a light as possible for all – again seeking the win/win.

This activity was not new to him, but he appreciated our thorough review of his influencing styles. The use of different aspects of non-verbal communication was an equally important point of discovery. A particular point which arose was his habit of looking away from the line of sight while talking – for instance when he had a difficult technical engineering point to convey to non-engineers. We discussed at length how to break down such habits. In part, this meant James learning how to get away from the detail – to be able to talk freely (and literally) directly to camera!

During this programme James usually knew 'what' he wanted to communicate but he found our discussion of the context and the 'how' invaluable. This allowed him to discover different ways of achieving his goals, and of seeing the different relative impacts of each way.

As a result of his determined and well-planned upward communication and managing of his consortium members, James received credit for surpassing his first year objectives. He did this in spite of the recasting of the original targets. In the light of the restructuring work he had brought to the board – and then exceeded even these higher, recast profit targets. Having communicated a lot of bad news to staff and his senior team earlier in the year, he was now able to share some successes with them, demonstrating the advantages of communicating both good *and* bad news to establish personal credibility and trust.

Though James and everyone at board level now understood each others' words and actions well, they at first failed to realize that they were a long way ahead of the rest of the organization and staff in their thinking and ability to adapt to new developments. We discussed this at length, often using the London Marathon as an analogy, as shown in Figure 7.2.

Professional runners start with a challenging time in mind. For them the London Marathon is merely one in a series – a preparation for the New York Marathon, which in turn will be a preparation for Sydney and so on. They, like James and his fellow board members, are way ahead in their thinking about goals, fitness, time constraints and so on, using the immediate experience to learn for the future. The way they talk amongst themselves will mean much more to avid marathon followers and keen athletes. They need to be careful to talk in different ways to other audiences with whom they wish to communicate their 'race to the goal'.

Amateur runners will run the same course, but their finishing goals are somewhat hazy and less urgent. They stick at them, but need to be more regularly fed and watered – and need more encouragement. They are like the Op Co managers who may aim to become board members in the end, but are not there yet.

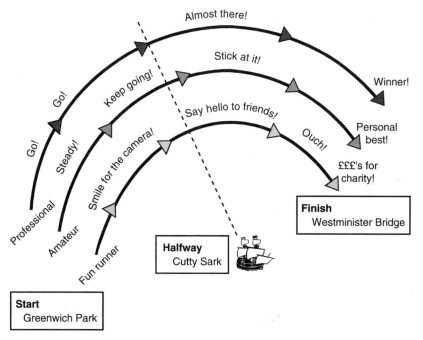

Figure 7.2 *Analogy of the London Marathon.*

They will be dedicated to this particular race but probably won't be thinking ahead to New York in mind. Such a distant goal does not help them – they need development to help them focus on the immediate race.

Going down a level, as it were, the 'fun runners' don't share the same criteria as the professionals or amateurs. They also follow the same course, but for an entirely different set of motives – to raise money, appear on television, publicize a good cause, or whatever. They are not motivated primarily by self-interest or ambition, and do not share the criteria by which the professionals' race will be judged. These are the long-serving employees who work in order to pay the mortgage, go out with friends, acquire new skills and gain new experience, but have no ambition to reach the very top. They need a localized, motivating form of communication that taps in to what matters to them.

This analogy helped James realize that he needed to communicate with people at their specific levels, because they have different motivations, levels of drive and states of awareness of the company's aims and objectives.

Reaching a Resolution

The principle lessons to be faced in meeting the challenge of communicating with all of the stakeholders all of the time are:

- How well do you understand your audience(s)? A full understanding is critical to good communication.

- Can you work out how to break the vicious circle of focusing on tasks to the detriment of communication, and avoid accusations that communication is lacking?

- Do you understand your key close relationships well enough to ensure success in those primary communications?

- Remember that, in any crisis, your feelings will be as much engaged as anyone else's, so rely on communicating facts more than feelings at times of crisis.

- Develop a controlled manner to put across your feelings – don't hide those feelings, but don't let them run amok either.

- Think through the other person's agenda, and seek win/win solutions – make a habit of this, and persevere. It's not easy!

- Think laterally to ensure that you create time to communicate – use all opportunities, including travel.

- Be visible to your people – this is an absolute necessity, not a 'nice to have', so work at it and check that you *are* visible.

- Flex your style to communicate well in each and every situation – each one is different … .

- Use your 'chain of command' to put messages across rapidly – and avoid the temptation (which will often arise!) to find short-cuts.

- Get ahead of the game by building scenarios to cover the major communication angles – and share these with your team, as this may give you a head start in a crisis.

- Analyse influencing styles – getting professional help as needed – and work out to add to your repertoire.

- Understand non-verbal communication and its power; and use it, as it can save a lot of words (and speech-writing).

- Realize that not everyone reads the same thing when you send an e-mail – there are very few shortcuts, so set out to communicate upward, sideways and downward.

- Communicate with people where they are, and as they are, remembering to factor in their knowledge base, attitudes, needs and viewpoints as you do so.

Chapter 8

Meeting the Diversity Challenge

Elizabeth Coffey

Context

I live in London and drive a car from Germany. British friends say that my steering column is 'on the wrong side'. My car is different from the norm, and therefore pronounced to have something 'wrong' with it! This trivial example ceases to be so when we accept how often people who look or behave unlike the norm are seen as less valid than the majority group. I have experienced many incidents of discrimination on the basis of my nationality (American) and gender – they energize me to work for positive change in the area of diversity discrimination.

What is culture? It is 'the way we do things', a manifestation of our norms and values expressed through language, food, architecture, dress, music, pace of life, public emotion, physical contact and work ethic. It is like gravity: you don't feel it unless you jump. It has been defined as 'the collective mental programming of a group of people',[1] and 'the way people respond to the challenges of time, nature, relationships and the general environment'.[2] Individuals are shaped by the cultures of, among others, their families, nations, ethnicities, organizations, functions and teams. Culture is so all-encompassing that it is hard to become fully aware of your own cultural assumptions. As a result, it is famously challenging to shift!

There are myriad diversity market drivers that could spur a CEO to change the culture of an organization. For example, ethnic minority customers might demand more tailored products or services, thereby shifting market expectations and leaving behind a company that fails to develop a more customer-focused culture. Or the company could lose a gender discrimination case, leading to a lambasting from the press and a boycott by customers. In both these cases, if the CEO doesn't react swiftly by introducing an appropriate culture change programme, damage to the company may be significant and long lasting.

Management bookshelves groan with models articulating how to create organizational change. These models often make the process look simple, but anyone who has led such an initiative knows that people resist change with all their might, particularly when it is being forced on them. The implementation of plans to shift culture is challenging and requires robust leadership from the top, corporate determination and absolute clarity about the business drivers spurring the change.

These rules apply to leading public sector organizations as well as to private companies.

Soon after Greg Dyke took on the role of Director-General at the BBC, he commented in a radio interview that the BBC was still 'hideously white'. This candid public remark signalled to both BBC employees and their customers Dyke's commitment to shifting the ethnic diversity within the BBC to reflect more accurately the licence-fee paying UK public, who constitute both their customer base and their funding body. In the months thereafter, listeners and viewers noticed a stronger presence of minority ethnic personnel and issues in BBC programmes. These visible changes reflect to BBC audiences ongoing wider shifts in the organizational internal culture which could:

- enhance the quality of programmes to connect with more diverse audiences
- indicate an inclusive culture within the BBC attractive to potential recruits and existing employees from under-represented backgrounds
- demonstrate to key stakeholders – like government – ethical use of public money.

In other words, some goals of the BBC's diversity initiatives are to increase their share of the market, improve their image as an employer of choice and strengthen their reputation for responsible use of resources amongst their regulators.

This chapter differs from the others: instead of describing the coaching of an individual CEO through a challenge, I describe our current work in creating diversity culture change across the UK Civil Service through a leadership development programme from the top down and the middle up. The work was sponsored by the Head of the Civil Service, Sir Richard Wilson, and his permanent secretaries. It was commissioned through the Cabinet Office's Learning and Strategy Division (LSD) and the government's Senior Advisor, Diversity Strategy & Equal Opportunities.

The programme can be used as a basis for culture change and developing 'high potentials' in any organization.

The initiative originated in the autumn of 1999 at the Civil Service Management College at Sunningdale. Sir Richard Wilson and the permanent secretaries agreed that it was imperative for them to improve government through a series of reforms. Among several strands, the Modernizing Government agenda highlights compelling reasons to develop the government approach to diversity and talent development.

Looking out to the customer base of the Civil Service – the tax-paying public – statistics illustrated that the diversity in the UK population was not reflected proportionally at the top of the Civil Service. Women, ethnic minorities, and the disabled were under-represented at Senior Civil Service (SCS) level. 'Where all think alike, no one thinks very much' said Walter Lippman. Research by Taylor Cox, Jr and others have supported that statement with hard data demonstrating that well-led, diverse teams outperform homogeneous teams by 15% or more.[3] This concept has significant ramifications for the government which is charged – by Prime Minister Tony Blair, in his second term in office – with delivering high-quality services to the whole of the UK public. Under-representation of a particular group within the leadership cadre impacts the variety and standard of services that group is offered.

Statistics indicate that there are approximately 7% ethnic minorities across the UK population (1999 data). In major cities, like London, the numbers are significantly higher (more than 30%). At the inception of the Modernizing Government initiatives, only 1.7% of the SCS came from ethnically diverse backgrounds (1998 data). Since London is the seat of central government, the low SCS ethnicity representation is glaring. These figures compare favourably with the private sector, where a recent study commissioned by the Runnymede Trust[4] identified that only 1% of FTSE-100 senior managers are ethnic minorities.

In the autumn of 2000, I was asked by the Cabinet Office to co-lead a team of Change Partnership colleagues in designing and delivering an innovative leadership development programme for talented middle management Civil Servants from ethnic minority backgrounds. The aim of this unique initiative was to begin to level the playing field for ethnic minorities by helping them to compete effectively for roles in the SCS, the top 3300 leadership positions within the organization. The Cabinet Office requested a two-year leadership development design for 20 participants annually. This will run for four consecutive years, so a total of 80 Civil Servants from ethnic minority backgrounds will benefit from two years of planned development to prepare them to compete for roles in the SCS. Over that time, three SCSs will work closely with each programme participant, initiating shifts in their skills, knowledge and awareness regarding diversity management. Individual shifts in behaviour will affect pockets of the Civil Service, cumulatively stimulating culture change in the SCS.

I believe that it is possible to generalize this specific model of developing high-potential employees into leadership roles in the Civil Service to other populations of talented employees, if it is tailored to suit their cultures. The Civil Service sponsors are keen to share this programme as a model of excellence.

Client Company Profile

The Civil Service Commission is one of the UK's largest employers, with 480,000 people across 150 departments and agencies. The top 1%, the Senior Civil Service, is renowned for attracting very bright graduates, but the organization is large, traditional and averse to taking undue risks, so promotions within its very hierarchical structure can take longer than in the private sector.

Due to its size, role and heritage, the Civil Service can seem to be slow to change. Each department has its own agenda, goals and style and, historically, there has been a tendency for departments to form isolated silos. In such a cautious and factionalized climate, an encompassing cross-department change initiative faces stiff and persistent resistance. Yet, the organization values the principles of fairness and meritocracy, and scores of people are working to join up the disparate departments and institute lasting reforms.

Client Profile

The 'client' is comprised of a wide variety of civil servants, from the Head of the Home Civil Service and Secretary of the Cabinet down. This programme has inspired the sponsorship of many leaders of the UK government, including Sir Richard Wilson, two key members of his management board (permanent secretaries Sir Nick Montagu and Robin Young) and many senior civil servants (grades 1–5).

The programme was commissioned by the Learning and Strategy Division of the Cabinet Office (John Barker and Liz Davis), and the government's Senior Advisor, Diversity Strategy & Equal Opportunities (Museji Takolia). We work closely with several Cabinet Office officials in ongoing implementation, especially Malcolm Horwill. At the core of this initiative, we are developing talented ethnic minority civil servants many of whom are at grade 6, grade 7 and specialist executive officer levels of the hierarchy. Our leadership development work touches all of these individuals.

The Challenge

'We could not tolerate being an organization where people are held back for reasons that have nothing to do with their qualities and abilities. And if we were, we would be cutting ourselves off from a pool of talent we can ill afford to neglect.' – 'Civil Service Reform', 2000

The management board of the Civil Service has ambitions to be an employer of choice: to be seen by UK civil servants, potential employees, private and public sector organizations, peer governments and the general public as leaders in the way they attract, retain and promote their people. A great deal has to change in order to achieve those ambitions, but a sharply defined organizational change initiative cannot succeed in isolation. As with a transplant, both the new organ (initiative) and the patient (organization) must be prepared if surgery is to be successful and organ rejection avoided.

Our challenge is to prepare the SCS for that 'surgery' and, simultaneously, to develop ethnic minority civil servants for 'transplant' into the SCS within the next five years. We need to create change in both groups for the overall culture shift to succeed.

Ours is one initiative in the overall Modernizing Government agenda, folded into a broader strategic framework under the dual headings of the Diversity agenda and the Bringing On Talent agenda, and it draws participants from across all departments of the Civil Service. There are two elements to the programme:

- Developing the leadership skills of high-potential civil servants from ethnic minority backgrounds.

- Changing the culture of the SCS to attract and retain these and future talented ethnically diverse leaders for the long term.

At the time of writing, we are one-quarter of the way through the development programme, and we are already seeing results.

Desired Results

To design and deliver a cutting edge programme that would:

- Prepare talented ethnic minorities to compete effectively for SCS positions within the next five years.

- Develop their leadership competencies and skills to the SCS Competency Framework.

- Raise the awareness about ethnicity issues across a significant cross-departmental population of the SCS.

- Stimulate 10% or more of the SCS to change the leadership climate at the top of the organization.

- Initiate a culture change in the SCS to ensure the promotion and long term retention of 3.2% ethnically diverse SCS peers by 2005.

The Developing Approach

By the time we were invited to lead this project, Sir Richard Wilson and Sir Nick Montagu had accomplished crucial planks of the accepted organizational culture change process. Their Modernizing Government document articulates:

- The key drivers for reform ('moral, business and social sense').

- Clear visionary targets (3.2% SCS ethnic minorities) and realistic time scales (by 2004/5).

- The current realities (1.7% SCS ethnic minorities in 1998).

- The gap between those realities and the vision.

- Management accountability for achieving all diversity targets within their divisions.

- Some guidelines for action planning (in the Civil Service Reform document).

They had already done the preliminary planning work for a culture change model. Our job was to pick up the reins and:

- Design a comprehensive tailored programme.

- Build support for it in the SCS and among ethnic minority Civil Servants.

- Implement the programme.

- Communicate constantly with all stakeholders throughout.

- Monitor and report progress.

Crafting the Draft Design

The following fundamental principles about large culture change informed the initial programme design:

- All change starts at the personal level.

- A fair proportion of senior individuals in a community must develop in a common direction to build momentum.

- People resist change. Start with passionate volunteers as the first agents of change.

- Success breeds success: once you have achieved positive profile in a change pilot, round up the next wave of energized volunteers to continue the work.

Gender and ethnic minority research consistently identifies that individuals labelled as 'different' from the norm are enabled and blocked in their careers by similar things. There are many ways in which women and ethnic minorities manifest difference from the majority: through the use of language, thinking styles, assumptions, motivations, and – of course – physical appearance. It is easy for the minority worker to become caught in the following downward cycle:

- make a 'different' suggestion for change which is shot down as 'wrong'

- become depressed and lose confidence

- lower horizons.

Enablers include encouragement from family, friends, colleagues and other professionals; guidance from role models, mentors and coaches; and achievement of high-profile roles.[5] UK government research in 2000 supported these findings, emphasizing the importance of line manager sponsorship and ethnically aligned role models.[6]

Ethnic minorities stem from very different backgrounds, cultures and religions yet are often lumped together by the majority. This causes resentment, as each person's or sub-group's needs vary widely. If these issues are not aired and resolved, mounting friction can threaten the group's cohesion and progress.

Since Clinton's administration in the White House had made great strides on diversity issues, I sought out knowledge of the US government senior executives' leadership development and diversity programmes to enrich design ideas. The US Equal Opportunities Commissioner and colleagues obliged my requests with reams of documents outlining the their innovative approaches.

The initial leadership development design incorporated excellent practices from all the above sources to maximize diversity enablers, overcome obstacles and cater for the specific needs of the group. It was built around the Government's levers for change for this programme:

● Passionate senior level sponsorship by Sir Richard Wilson and Sir Nick Montagu.

● Clearly articulated drivers for the changes (in the Civil Service Reform document).

● Sharply-focused managerial targets and accountability.

● Realistic timeframes.

● Talented and ambitious ethnic minority civil servants to drive the initiative.

● Forward thinking members of the SCS, ready to volunteer to support it.

Pathways Phase One

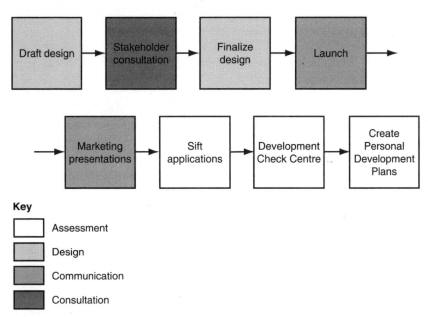

Figure 8.1 *Pathways phase one: design, communication, assessment.*

Stakeholder Consultation and Final Design

With a two-year draft development design in hand, our Change Partnership team of 10 carried out a comprehensive stakeholder consultation with 65 senior civil servants, members of the ethnic minority community within and beyond the Civil Service (CS), and trade union leaders. At these meetings, we asked:

- What is the climate for change in ethnic minority development?

- What previous initiatives have worked – or not worked – and why?

- What has your personal experience of these initiatives been?

- What enablers and blockers are there for ethnic groups?

- What do you think of our initial design?

The answers enabled us to:

- Raise awareness of the initiative across an important group of stakeholders.

- Enable those stakeholders to help shape the initiative and act as informal ambassadors for it.

- Unearth potential trouble spots, and identify sensitivities regarding use of language, cross-departmental working and political agendas.

After this lengthy 'evidence gathering' exercise we honed the design accordingly.

We heard repeatedly that any centrally initiated (Cabinet Office) programme would need to be owned and flavoured by each department involved with it. Therefore, departmental stakeholder involvement would need to be more active and regular than we had imagined. As part of this, we were told that the programme's name might be changed by any department in order to brand it, so we chose a neutral, flexible yet evocative name – Pathways – that emphasized the choices people have in determining which roads to follow in their careers.

Since communication between departments and agencies was imperfect at best, we found we needed to take a more active role in this than we had planned. In addition, work exposure – managed postings, work placements, secondments, job shadowing – raised an individual's profile in the Civil Service more than we had expected, so we placed stronger emphasis on this.

One of the most surprising findings was the importance the SCS placed on the precise use of language. For example, there was a lengthy debate about whether this should be termed a 'programme', a 'project', a 'scheme' or an 'initiative'. We were astonished by the vigour with which our stakeholders addressed this (to us) peripheral point! Another sign of how important it would be to tailor our programme to the organization's cultural sensitivities.

Launch and Marketing Presentations

We launched Pathways with Sir Nick Montagu and Robin Young at a widely publicized and well-attended event at the Cabinet Office. The launch was immediately followed by two weeks of marketing events, presenting the design and inviting questions from cross-departmental audiences, including Civil Service ethnic minority networks, HR professionals, diversity advisors and potential SCS mentors. We spoke with about 1000 civil servants around the UK.

The question-and-answer sessions following the presentations were challenging, with the ethnic minority audience cynical about 'yet another' well-intentioned government initiative. At the end of it all I could have faced a live inquisition from Jeremy Paxman or Diane Sawyer.

Applications Sift and Development Check Centre

On the back of these marketing efforts, and a Pathways website, we received applications from more than 90 civil servants – self-nominated or nominated by another. My colleague, Dr Donald McLeod, led the next phase of the programme in assessing and choosing the participants. As some psychometric instruments are renowned for their bias against ethnic minorities, this was a highly sensitive phase. Donald designed a watertight Development Check Centre (DCC), anticipating a great deal of scrutiny. He led a team of Change Partnership colleagues and civil servant assessors to sift 61 candidates from 91 applicants for the one-day DCC.

The robust SCS Competency Framework, 'Leadership for Results', has six prime components (fleshed out through ample behavioural detail, omitted here for simplicity):

1. Giving purpose and direction (creating and communicating a vision of the future).

2. Making a personal impact (leading by example).

3. Thinking strategically (harnessing ideas and opportunities to achieve goals).

4. Getting the best from people (motivating and developing people to achieve high performance).

5. Learning and improving (drawing on experience and new ideas to improve results).

6. Focusing on delivery (achieving value for money and results).

The application form design was novel in asking the candidates to assess themselves against these dimensions. Donald's team hosted 12 groups of five candidates, who were scored according to this DCC version of the Competency Model on: paper-based personality instrument (Orpheus, a work-based questionnaire specifically designed to avoid bias); a cognitive test (the GMA Abstract, also designed to reduce differential impact); an in-tray exercise; a group discussion; and a one-to-one interview.

Based on numerical scorings, the assessors narrowed the field to 21. Each of the 61 candidates received one to two hours of personal feedback on strengths and areas for improvement against the Competency Framework. This discussion (and accompanying documentation) formed the basis for each candidate's Personal Development Plan (PDP). Our colleagues at the LSD, who had observed each of the DCCs, reported that the feedback on the process from all candidates – successful and otherwise – was glowing. Our assessment team created a group profile *vis-à-vis* the Competency Framework which we used to tailor the away days.

Pathways Phase Two

Development Design

The approved design outlined that, during a two-year period of varied personalized development plans – including Away Days, work exposure, coaching and mentoring (see Fig. 8.2) – participants would be prepared to compete for SCS roles. Over the course of the development, they would:

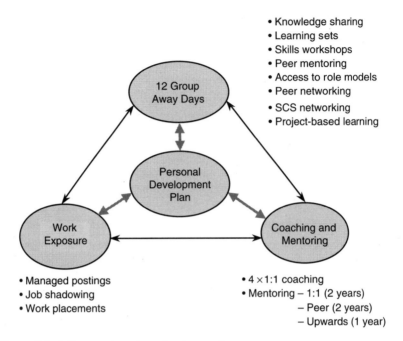

Figure 8.2 *Pathways phase two: development.*

- Learn about the culture of the SCS.

- Develop the skills and competencies required by the Competency Framework.

- Build relationships with SCS mentors, role models and mentees, through one-on-one mentoring, networking events and planned work experiences.

- Increase their understanding of the overt and subtle processes which determine access to the SCS.

- Develop confidence.

In conjunction, SCS line managers, mentors and mentees would develop their understanding of the Civil Service's ethnic diversity through:

- diversity and mentoring briefings

- an induction course

- shaping participants' PDPs

- a one- to two-year mentoring relationship

- reviewing progress of the participants (ongoing and annual).

This design affects culture in three ways. Firstly, as the Pathways participants are promoted into the SCS, their unique viewpoints will influence its culture and policies. Secondly, in parallel, through personal involvement, senior stakeholders become more aware of the issues faced by ethnic minorities and reconsider their own assumptions and their thoughts on acceptable behaviours and practices. These individual adjustments will, with time, transform team and peer expectations, affect policy and evolve the culture. Thirdly, over its six-year lifetime, Pathways will involve about 300 leaders (10%). Through dialogue with peers, these leaders will cascade learning, influencing their colleagues' thinking and behaviours. This will gradually engender a more inclusive leadership culture.

Diversity and Mentoring Briefings

Malcolm Horwill, of the LSD, brought us a list of volunteer SCS mentors, whom we screened by telephone. Research shows that line managers are the biggest enablers or blockers to ethnic minority career advancement, so we needed to engage their support, too. We invited line managers and mentors to a mandatory half-day briefing on diversity. The purpose of this event was to:

- clarify the practical implications of Pathways

- reinforce their importance in making it successful

- align our expectations about their roles in the process

- provoke thought about:

- what the SCS could gain by encouraging diversity in its ranks

- what sensitive issues might arise in the course of the programme

- how the SCS could work to create an inclusive culture

- the leadership skills required to manage diversity effectively.

My colleague, Tony Montes, and I showed the group a short film illustrating diversity issues, stimulating individual, small group and plenary discussions around these topics. We encouraged dialogue about how minority survivors typically cope with being different: assimilating to the host culture, stimulating evolution in it, or sparking revolution! Through Pathways, participants need to develop acceptable levels of SCS skills and capabilities, while retaining the distinctiveness which will enrich the mix and evolve the culture.

Several remarked that they had found the briefing 'surprisingly thought provoking ... leaving more questions than answers about ethnic minority diversity and the SCS'. Their determination to support Pathways was obvious.

Next, we conducted a half-day briefing for the selected mentors to outline: mentoring skills and how the mentoring process should work; the recommended frequency and duration of meetings; the potential mentoring requirements of ethnic minorities.

Through this interactive session, we heard that the mentors anticipated learning a great deal from their mentees. This group seemed highly committed and sophisticated in their approach.

Induction

Participants came together for the first time at the induction in November 2001. During the evening, coaches and SCS colleagues celebrated with the participants their success in attaining places on Pathways. Sir Richard Wilson, who sponsored Pathways from its inception, inspired the group with a heartfelt speech.

The next morning, we briefed participants on mentoring to align their expectations about this two-year commitment with the mentors'. I matched mentoring pairs by linking individuals in similar geographical regions and working in different departments who were, where possible, of opposite genders (just to throw a little more diversity learning into the mix!). We gave the pairs 90 minutes to get to know each other informally. Over lunch, we introduced the line managers to the mentoring pairs to establish three-way partnerships. Then, we outlined Pathways to the group, emphasizing the critical role each stakeholder would play in its success.

A disturbing situation arose that emphasized the wisdom of involving line managers so strongly in the programme from the start. Just before the induction, one participant was promoted and, consequently, got a new line manager. This (white) woman, recently promoted into the SCS had not attended the diversity briefing and so had no understanding of Pathways. She expressed her displeasure at sacrificing a day for this new direct report, and publicly accused him of wasting her time. She had a long way to travel in terms of her commitment to and understanding of diversity issues. This had probably been the case with other line managers, but they had not had to begin their journeys in public.

The situation was managed vigorously and rapidly. The sponsors, facilitators, mentor and coach took immediate action to protect the participant. A Cabinet Office official wrote to the line manager (and her boss), outlining the day's incidents and requesting a formal apology to the participant. The Cabinet Office helped the line manager and her boss come to an understanding of the issue. Her apology came promptly. In the following months, sponsors spoke regularly with the participant, and his mentor and coach supported him through the subtle lingering effects of the initial clash.

At an away day four months later participants reported that they were receiving either passive or active support from all the managers we had briefed. In contrast, several participants who had changed jobs in the intervening months were experiencing resistance from their new managers. To accommodate successive waves of new managers, we augmented the programme design to include a rolling series of diversity briefings throughout its tenure.

Group Away Days

My colleagues, Sue Godfrey and Tony Montes, and I tailored the away days to reflect the group profile *vis-à-vis* the Competency Framework. We hosted them every two months off-site, and each event included:

- An invited SCS dinner speaker as role model, inspiration and senior networking contact.

- Project group work focused on ethnicity issues and the CS, to foster working in teams and learning about group dynamics, managing limited resources under pressure, and adding value back into the CS while raising their profiles.

- Learning sets for peer mentoring.

- Exercises to build leadership skills and competencies.

- Sharing success stories.

We recognized that there was great variety in the backgrounds and personalities of the group members, so we took an hour on the second away day to share their experiences of being ethnic minorities in the Civil Service. The exercise forged bonds between them.

A Cambridge-educated man with two postgraduate degrees, whose parents were immigrants from the Indian sub-continent, had been born and raised in England. He was invited to stay with a friend, a middle class, white, suburban English woman. One of her relatives said, surprised and congratulatory, 'you speak such good English!' Nineteen years later, he was speaking at a conference. Another delegate, impressed by his eloquence and clarity, commented in a shocked tone 'you spoke really well!', exposing his low expectations.

As the stories collected, individuals began to refer to the experiences of others in the room. The last person to speak, a naturally upbeat man, wondered – in light of others' reflections – whether he had refused to allow himself to believe that he could be discriminated against at work. The stories had made him reframe previous experiences.

Work Exposure

Already, several participants have shadowed senior individuals, gaining valuable insights and raising their profiles. To identify tailored managed postings and work placements to suit participants' career aspirations takes time. Line managers, mentors and coaches are outlining participants' specific requirements and unearthing appropriate opportunities for them. Soon, participants will move into three- to six-month placements and postings, boosting their profiles at senior level in targeted departments.

Monitoring Progress

On an individual basis, changes became visible within a couple of months of the induction. In one case, just two coaching sessions produced dramatic results. At our first meeting, Rilesh Jadeja spoke of a recent professional situation in which he had lacked confidence, so we devoted that session to defining and acknowledging his strengths, skills and capabilities. At our next meeting, we used a 30-minute memory and discovery exercise to develop his confidence.

When we met the third time, Rilesh appeared taller, held his head higher. He announced that he had achieved a promotion, and exuded quiet pride. After relaying the detail about his new job, he told me that me that the coaching had affected his life deeply. 'I like myself more,' he said. 'I feel valuable. I have more confidence.'

Rilesh was not the only participant who found the coaching valuable in building his sense of self-esteem. Many similar stories filtered back to me, citing the coaches as instrumental in helping participants achieve promotions, land senior job-shadowing opportunities and secure meetings with Permanent Secretaries. These tales underscored the supreme importance of confidence in raising the horizons of the participants and spurring them to manage their careers proactively. Several stated that the coaching was the single most effective developmental intervention in Pathways; they asked for more!

In the second year, each participant will be 'upward mentoring' a volunteer from the SCS about the experience of being an ethnic minority in the Civil Service. He or she will thus develop a coaching style of leadership while engaging more ambassadors for culture change through Pathways. Now, our professional coaches and the mentors are role modelling those skills.

Three months into the mentoring, we telephoned all 42 mentors and mentees to check progress on the chemistry, process, frequency and duration of meetings, and how they were managing differing expectations. Responses were uniformly positive. Many mentors spoke of how they had discussed broader diversity issues with their mentees, soliciting their perspectives on departmental equal opportunities policies, managing harassment, etc. Mentors were facilitating strategic senior introductions and hosting job shadowing for their mentees themselves. One mentee and his mentor swapped management tips and were developing what promised to be a long-term friendship.

One year into Pathways, each participant will review progress against his PDP with his line manager and mentor. Together, they will reshape the PDP to reflect achievements against the original aims and shifts in the goalposts for the second year of development. At the end of the second year, this process will be repeated to evaluate and celebrate successes as Pathways concludes.

The facilitators monitor the group's progress at each away day through observation and group discussion. We solicit written and verbal feedback for each session, and tweak designs to reflect the current priorities, mood and pace of the group, so the participants are co-creating their group learning experience.

Cabinet Office sponsorship changes were visible, too. Initially, there had been concern about how Pathways would be perceived by other departments, but the overwhelming enthusiasm elicited by the launch and marketing spread around the Civil Service and back to Cabinet Office sponsors. This prompted them to take Pathways to a wider audience, and grant an interview to a broadsheet newspaper about it. Two months ago, Sir Nick Montagu spoke to 50 private and public sector diversity experts about Pathways' success and The Change Partnership's stewardship of it.

The LSD now receives a stream of positive feedback about Pathways; government leaders are clamouring to 'touch' the programme by speaking at Away Days. The third one attracted five guest leaders rather than the usual one; our most visible sponsor, Sir Richard Wilson, made his final Pathways appearance before his retirement. We have hosted three away days over six months, and the success stories pour in each time: almost half the participants have achieved promotions that take them closer to achieving their ambitions.

We are witnessing changes, too, in the SCS climate. Last year Suma Chakrabarti was promoted into a management board position: the first ethnic minority in UK history to attain a permanent secretary role. Since Pathways began, ethnic minority representation in the SCS has risen from 1.7% to 2.4%. Annual monitoring will provide a statistical yardstick for progress.

Now, as we launch Pathways Two, the LSD is much more assured about the process, time scales and people we must involve at various stages. Pathways participants are speaking at marketing events, adding credibility as role models for potential candidates and providing insider evaluations of the programme. Pleasingly, a surprisingly high percentage of audience members have been asked by their line managers to apply to Pathways Two!

Pathways is manifestly succeeding in its aims of:

- Enhancing leadership capability, raising participants' profiles and levels of confidence, and increasing their awareness of SCS norms and culture.

- Driving culture change in the SCS, thus and through the personal engagement of its leaders Already, this is increasing stakeholders' awareness of colleagues' behaviours and inspiring discussion.

Over the lifetime of Pathways we hope to create 330 agents of culture change, a very potent force with a passion to germinate a culture that embraces and celebrates the diversity in its ranks.

Reaching a Resolution

Any diversity culture change programme should address these questions thoroughly:

- What does your organization need to do to serve your diverse customer base effectively? Demonstrate that the percentages of diverse leaders are reflective of the customer community? Augment products or services to delight diverse customers?

- How can you demonstrate an inclusive culture to attract and retain the best talent? What are your leaders doing that discourages diversity? How can you provide the senior role models needed to show that real opportunities for advancement exist for diverse talent?

- What is the best way to nurture and promote talented individuals? What mix of sophisticated career planning, mentoring, senior sponsorship, leadership development programmes, skills and competencies development, external coaching and diversity education is right for your company?

- How can you leverage different perspectives to enhance innovation? Map your future markets and the demographic realities. Work out how your diverse talent can maximize new opportunities.

- What are achievable targets and timeframes in making these changes? Identify short-, medium- and long-term goals in specific and measurable chunks.

- How can you create management accountability for achieving the diversity culture change goals? How will you measure individual success and failure, and how frequently?

- What kinds of reward systems will be effective in spurring change? Regular celebration of success? Annual assessments on diversity performance targets? Discretionary bonuses or increased chances for promotion?

- How can you ensure regular communication and reinforcement from senior sponsors?

I feel so at home here – y'all speak American!

Chapter 9

Surviving in the Global Jungle

Bob Goodall

Context

We live in a global market place, or so we are constantly told. The opportunities waiting for us all in that market can tempt the most level headed of business people. We also live in times in which the name of the game is growth. The business leaders who hit the headlines are those who achieve great growth – and they often hit them at least twice, once on the way up and once on the way down! The leader who runs a steady ship and looks for continuity rather than growth doesn't usually merit a mention. It's hardly surprising, then, that more and more companies are being drawn beyond their national boundaries in the search for new markets and major expansion. But be warned: international expansion brings with it strategic, organizational and cultural complexities, not to mention a heavy toll on personal time.

The strategic issues are very company-specific. However, whatever your business, the product or service and marketing strategies will become many times more complex once you cross national boundaries. New questions emerge. Should the product or service be redesigned to meet local market requirements, potentially sacrificing economies of scale and demanding an in-depth knowledge of local markets? Or can one product or service be designed for all markets? This latter approach is feasible; we only have to look at the way McDonald's overcame the aversion to fast food in many parts of continental Europe by linking their product to an international youth culture. However, it does incur the need for massive marketing support to break down national prejudices and preferences.

Then there are the international anti-globalization pressure groups to contend with which, at the very least, may require a significant PR effort if you are not to be diverted from your preferred strategic direction. As I write, in the light of violence in Geneva and Genoa, *The Times* headline reads: 'Brussels police put on riot alert for EU Summit'. The anti-globalization movement is relatively new. It took off at the 1999 Seattle meeting of the World Trade Organization and 200,000 demonstrators disrupted the Genoa G8 Summit in July 2001.

The movement may be new, but international pressure groups are not. I witnessed this first-hand in the early 1990s when with Inchcape plc. We had a thriving timber business but suffered continuing pressure from the environmentalists who oppose any further felling of the rain forest. It is easy to sympathize with their position on the one hand, but Inchcape was a very responsible forester, limiting its felling to approved guidelines and replanting diligently. Notwithstanding this, the decision was taken to exit the timber business because of negative PR. It was sold to a local South-east Asian company. They would certainly be less concerned by Western environmental pressure groups, and it is questionable that they would be as responsible in their care for the rainforest as Inchcape had been. Whatever, our international strategy was changed in response to persistent and, in this case, effective lobbying.

Building the right structure is a critical ingredient of the success of any business. But that becomes much more difficult once you cross those national borders, as the Stopford and Wells 'International Structural Stages Model' demonstrates.[1] Their model suggests that the appropriate structure changes as the scale and complexity of international operations increase:

International division	=	Overseas sales and product diversity low
Regional structure	=	Overseas sales and product diversity medium
Global matrix	=	Overseas sales and product diversity high

Sounds simple, but wherever you are on the model there are some hairy issues waiting. The International Division at the home-country headquarters is easily established and managed; but, as Stopford and Wells point out, how do you overcome uni-dimensional perspectives and management biases resultant from national culture? For its part, the global matrix sounds logically compelling, but is it manageable? The managers in the individual countries, 'country managers', struggle to retain their autonomy while 'global product managers' seek to establish control and legitimacy. It is hardly surprising that relationships in such a matrix are frequently adversarial.

If you are about to embark on the international adventure, maintaining a balance between business, geographic and functional management capabilities will become a significant challenge for you.

Even if you get the structure right, you still have to deal with national culture. It's only a short train ride from London to Paris but the two cities feel like different worlds. Once your business crosses national borders, how to respond to very different traditions, histories and management styles must be high on your agenda. It requires a sensitive touch, not something for which every go-getting business leader is renowned!

One thing is common to all cultures: local interest will be placed above global interest. In *Managing Across Borders,* Bartlett and Ghoshal[2] argue that to manage successfully internationally we need to reverse the traditional change process – see Figure 9.1.

Quite a challenge. Are you still sure you want to cross that border?

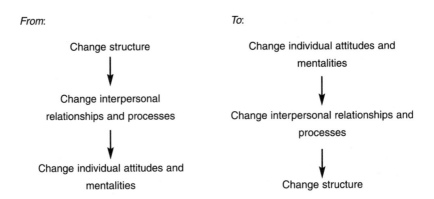

Figure 9.1 *Reversing the traditional change process.*

The lifestyle of an international manager may sound glamorous to friends at the golf club, but the reality is very different. Forget getting your handicap down for a kick-off. You may end up leaving home on a Sunday lunchtime to catch an afternoon flight; returning on Friday evening, with the flight delayed an hour and held a further 30 minutes over Heathrow by air traffic control. The glamour soon wears off. There are many compensations of course: you will meet wonderful people, explore fascinating cultures and face complex challenges – but never underestimate the importance of managing your personal life carefully if you are going to go international.

At the time of writing, we are a few months past the terrible 11 September destruction in New York and Washington. It is too early to tell what the consequences of these events, and the subsequent 'War on Terrorism', will be for international management. What impact this will have on other economies around the world and what it will do for the international strategies of businesses, is yet to unfold. This is not the only question. On the personal level, how will business executives respond to the increasing and now ever-present threat of terrorism? Certainly, in its immediate aftermath, Americans lost their appetite for international travel. For the tourist, that is a matter of choice. For the businessman it is not so simple – and may result in a reappraisal of how best to run an international business.

The sponsoring company for the coaching programme I describe was initially UK-based and owned but, shortly after my work began, it was acquired by a US company. This programme shows what it is like to be acquired by an organization in its attempt to globalize. In this context, coach and client sought to resolve the strategic, organizational, cultural and personal issues outlined above.

The Client Company

Jefferson Inc. is a US-based company employing 7000 staff around the world with an international turnover of $1.6 billion. Jefferson started life as a manufacturing company in New Jersey and moved overseas in the 1960s to take advantage of lower manufacturing costs. Opportunities for vertical expansion led to the acquisition of several new businesses over the years. Jefferson now operates in 20 countries, with particularly strong presence in South America and Europe, in addition to its home North American market. It operates in a number of business sectors: electrical goods, electrical components, retailing, testing services, financial services. In 2001, Jefferson bought a medium-sized component manufacturing company in the UK, Comsort Limited. In so doing it doubled the scale of its component manufacturing business world-wide.

The Client

Richard May had been appointed CEO of Comsort Limited in 1999, six months before its acquisition by Jefferson. Richard had been with the company for some years, latterly as Manufacturing Director. Sixty per cent of Comsort's shares were still held by the founding family. Richard had approached me to help him work on the wider leadership implications of a CEO role. Two months after the coaching programme started, the family sold all its shares to Jefferson Inc. and Comsort was taken over.

The Challenge

The challenge was a straightforward one: Richard had to demonstrate his leadership, both to the new owners and to the unsettled Comsort management team, from day one.

The challenge was compounded by the fact that Richard did not know enough about the Jefferson business, its products, structure and culture, to make rapid judgements. At the strategic level one thing was clear: Jefferson wanted to assimilate Comsort into its parent structure as quickly as possible, and to use it as the vehicle for European expansion. The major problem facing Richard was that Jefferson's component business was not large relative to their other operations and was in many ways dissimilar to the Comsort business.

Jefferson was organized into Global Business Divisions, all running out of the US headquarters. In terms of the Stopford and Wells model, this was effectively the equivalent of an international division for each business within Jefferson.

The organizational challenges and responses emerged as the coaching progressed. What was very quickly apparent, however, was that Richard would have to work hard to keep his own executive team motivated. Stan Pilgrim, an American, had been in the Global VP role for about 18 months. That had given him some international exposure in South America. His previous experience had been exclusively in the USA. His cultural sensitivity was not high – for Stan, a common language indicated a common culture: the British team would do it the American way.

And one final challenge soon became apparent: opportunities were definitely there for Richard if he could successfully position Comsort within Jefferson, but Jefferson's top management were US based with global remits requiring extensive travel. Richard's family situation, a working wife and three young children, meant that he was not internationally mobile or, indeed, anxious for major international responsibilities.

The Desired Results

● To maintain the motivation of the Comsort management team and develop them into appropriate positions in Jefferson's Global Components Division.

● To ensure that Jefferson understood the specific customer requirements in the UK components business and that this business was safeguarded and developed.

● To develop with Jefferson an appropriate strategy for expansion in Continental Europe.

● To develop a career strategy that would enable Richard to succeed within Jefferson while keeping his UK base and general management responsibilities.

The Developing Approach

Richard advised me of the take over and a forthcoming meeting with Stan Pilgrim, the VP Global Components, who would be overseeing the integration process. Richard was feeling low. He had been excited at achieving his first CEO position and confident that he could make a major contribution to Comsort, but now his general management aspirations were threatened.

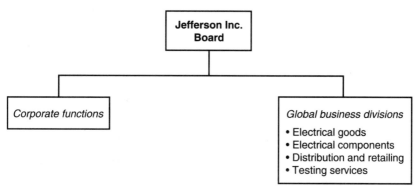

Figure 9.2 *Jefferson Inc.*

Richard told me that Jefferson was organized into Global Business Divisions, all running out of the US headquarters. In terms of the Stopford and Wells model, this was effectively the equivalent of an International Division for each business within Jefferson. Stan Pilgrim, the Global VP Components, was working quickly to incorporate Comsort into this Global Division.

I spent the early part of the session focusing Richard on the opportunities Jefferson might offer him and his team, rather than the threats to his personal career development. This was largely to put him in a positive frame of mind for his meeting with Stan. It would have been appropriate in any circumstances, but my previous experience with US corporate culture suggested that it would be even more so in the case of an American parent, where a can-do attitude would mandatory.

The remainder of the session was devoted to discussing how Richard should handle the first meeting. His inclination was to allow Stan to take the lead, but I suggested that it might be more appropriate for him to do so as he could then determine the agenda. We considered what information he had on Stan's background and what that might tell us about the things that would be of most interest to him. We looked at what information was available on the organizational structure employed by Jefferson, which was limited but sufficient to tell us that the seat of power was in the USA and the case for retaining a strong local focus in the UK would need to be carefully prepared. Finally, we considered what Stan's expectations were likely to be for this first meeting and concluded that a better understanding of Comsort should be top of his list. We decided to use the first meeting to impress upon Stan as firmly as possible Comsort's excellence in the UK market and the strength of its team. Richard went away with the task of preparing a presentation covering Comsort's vision, market, products, financials, structure and people.

Richard's first meeting with Stan went very well. Stan listened, asked questions and declared himself impressed with the presentation and the team. Importantly from Richard's perspective, he had not prematurely announced any strategic or structural initiatives that it might have been difficult to reverse at a later stage. Our first aim had therefore been achieved: we had discouraged Stan from taking positions before he understood the Comsort business.

Richard advised me that Stan had established a task force on the future organizational structure for component manufacturing. We knew that Jefferson organized all its business into Global Product Groups based in the USA and supported by Regional Managers in the field. The structure appeared on the surface to suggest two predictable concerns, namely the uni-dimensional perspectives and management biases of international divisions, and the conflicts between global and regional roles; and one very unusual one – no national managers.

This worried Richard enormously, particularly as the UK components business represented 50% of Jefferson's total. In his view, the demands of the UK component market were very different from those of others served by Jefferson. Comsort enjoyed excellent, long-standing relationships with its customers and a reputation for outstanding customer service. He feared these would be lost.

He also had concerns on a personal level: he had only been CEO for six months and now feared he would lose the title before he had had an opportunity to establish his credentials as a general manager. He did not want a global role or regional role for family reasons and saw himself returning to a national manufacturing role or having to leave.

Richard wanted to air his personal and professional concerns to Stan. I suggested that it was a mistake to combine business and personal agendas: by declaring his unwillingness, for family reasons, to take a global or regional role, he would be bound to taint his argument in Stan's eyes and detract from the validity of the business case.

Before going any further, we looked at the strength of Richard's argument for treating the UK as a unique market. I was concerned that he was displaying the usual tendency to put local considerations ahead of global, and argue for 'his' country to be treated as an exception to the norm. Richard was able to demonstrate that there were very special regulations which did indeed distinguish the UK market from the non-European component markets in which Jefferson was currently active (i.e. North and South America). I pointed out that these same arguments would not hold water in the cases of the European markets in which Jefferson operated, albeit on a relatively small scale, and so did not constitute a case against treating the UK as part of a European regional structure.

We used the rest of the session to consider how he would best influence the evolving organizational structure for global components. I reminded him that Stan had set up a task force, so nothing was set in stone, even if there was a bias in favour of the Global Product Manager/Regional Manager model. We looked at its composition and found that the task force was heavily biased in favour of those with global or functional accountabilities, and Jefferson rather than Comsort personnel. I suggested that, in these circumstances, the outcome of a head-on win/lose strategy was fairly obvious – Richard would lose. He needed, therefore, to promote a win/win strategy – enhanced local focus within a global components structure. I recommended he read *Managing Across Borders* by

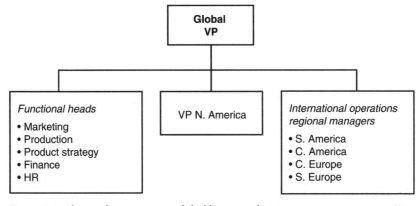

Figure 9.3 *Electrical components: global business division.*

Bartlett and Ghoshal, feeling that its combination of empirical learning and practical case studies would help him to marshal his arguments.

By our next session, Richard had done his homework thoroughly, championed with the task force what we had seen as a win/win strategy of local focus within a global components structure, and lost the day! The task force had recommended that Jefferson continue to apply its normal structure of Global Product Managers and Regional Support teams.

Richard was depressed and, when communicating the outcome to the Comsort management team, found morale dangerously low. But there was good news too: the task force had recommended that an integration team be established to consider how to make the structure work in the UK. I spent the early part of the session persuading Richard to see this as an opportunity and a signal that Stan had taken on board his concerns for the UK business.

We decided that there would be three major themes for the remainder of the session:

- How best to look after the UK business in the short term (12 months) until Jefferson had a chance to appreciate the very different nature of the UK market.

- How best to support his team and rebuild morale.

- How to influence the structuring of his own role.

I pointed out to Richard that Jefferson was making the mistake highlighted by Bartlett and Ghoshal: they were following the traditional change process and starting from structure, without addressing individual attitudes and mentalities. I suggested that, in the circumstances, it was incumbent on Richard to address these within his executive team, first allaying their fears about security – it is difficult to develop positive attitudes when people think their jobs are at risk.

As regarded his own position, Richard wanted to retain the UK CEO role for at least 12 months, feeling that this would be sufficient time to enable him to protect the position of UK customers. He was not interested in any of the global functional roles because of the travel involved and the problems that would create in his family. I suggested that in discussions with Stan he focus on the former argument: US companies operating internationally expect mobility from senior executives and are unlikely to have much sympathy for a reluctance to move or travel extensively.

As a first step, I suggested he should ensure as many of his team as possible were actively involved with the integration team, and that he and his executive team continue to pursue a win/win strategy of local focus within the global structure.

At our next meeting, Richard was back to his former optimistic self and felt he was making significant progress. He had worked hard with his executive team, individually and collectively, and morale was improving. All were closely involved with the integration team, and the task force was becoming increasingly receptive to the need for local emphasis, at least in the short term, in the UK. Meanwhile Stan had offered Richard a joint portfolio – Global VP, Product Strategy and Regional Manager, North Europe.

Richard was happy about the product strategy role, as he felt Comsort was well ahead of Jefferson in this area, and, of all the global functional roles, it was the one that would require the least travel. Jefferson would be happy for him to maintain his UK base and to combine it with the regional role. The role played to Richard's technical strengths, and would probably only require six visits to the USA a year plus an annual trip around the South American and European operations.

On the downside, the regional role covered not only the UK, but also Benelux (Belgium, the Netherlands and Luxembourg) and Scandinavia. The components business in the given area was small and Richard felt the opportunity there to be limited. To do the job properly would require extensive travel and take Richard's eye off the vastly more significant UK market.

We spent much of the session examining the two roles in detail. The first was manageable. The real problem was the inclusion of Benelux and Scandinavia in the regional role.

I suggested that Stan was trying to accommodate Richard as best he could. He had probably added Benelux and Scandinavia precisely because they were not seen as significant, at least in the short-term, allowing Richard to focus on the UK. We agreed that Richard would try to persuade Stan that the UK market, because of its significance to Jefferson, should be treated as a region in its own right, at least for the first year. By moving Benelux and Scandinavia into one of the other European regions and managing the UK alone, Stan could maintain the integrity of the global/regional matrix while meeting Richard's requirements.

Richard returned with excellent news. Stan agreed the proposed structure as an interim measure: for the next 12 months Richard and his team could focus on the UK market. As a bonus, as Global VP Product Strategy, Richard could influence the global components strategy and hence strategic developments that would impact on the UK market.

Richard was also delighted because his UK HR Director had advised him that the executive team had held together during the fraught six-month period after the acquisitions largely because of their collective loyalty to Richard. We discussed the success he had enjoyed in getting the team behind him, and also the opportunity he now had to further develop the team. His own dual role meant that he would only have half of his time to focus on the UK. He needed, therefore, to assess his team and increase the level of delegation. We discussed the extent to which the members were ready for this and I suggested that Richard did not have to increase their scope in a uniform manner. He could, instead, direct his support where it was most needed.

We then discussed how the organizational structure was likely to develop longer-term. The agreement to treat the UK as a region was a concession to Richard as much as recognition that there were unique features in that market. Since it might not last beyond the agreed time, it was imperative that Richard should use the 12 months to change the culture of Comsort.

The problems he had faced were only partly due to the fact that Jefferson had been wedded to a particular structure and had, initially at least, placed structure before the other critical change stages. Comsort's very UK-centric culture and tendency to see everything in the UK as unique had been contributory factors. While it was true that there were huge differences between the Jefferson businesses in the UK and the Americas, there was also considerable scope for common development.

We opened a discussion on how Richard could start to develop an international outlook in his executive team. This meant working with the team, individually and collectively, to change mindsets. An excellent starting place would be highlighting the enhanced career development opportunities that the new parent offered them. We looked at the positive aspects that Richard could see, having been exposed to Jefferson's management culture more than the rest of the team: international markets; increased resources (financial and human); a determination to expand and the capital resources to do so; and a strong interest in developing people.

Richard also recognized that Jefferson's components business was in many ways unlike Comsort's. He and his team were only too aware of the threats this created, but were not focusing on the opportunities it afforded. Richard acknowledged that, because he himself was not attracted to an international career, he had failed to enthuse his team with the positive prospects Jefferson offered, and now went away determined to do so. We agreed that one effective method would be to expose his team to Jefferson in the States, so Richard determined to find opportunities to get all of his direct reports over to Jefferson's corporate headquarters within the next three months.

In business we learn that things rarely happen exactly as planned, especially where people are involved! Richard next reported that the formal announcement of the revised organization had omitted any mention of his continuing role as regional manager for the UK.

Instead it said that he would become VP, Global Product Strategy but would continue to oversee the UK on a temporary basis until alternative arrangements had been agreed.

Richard was extremely upset and said that he had lost faith in Stan. He had a forthcoming trip to the USA and was keen to confront Stan on the issue.

To take the heat out of the situation, I suggested that we first try to establish why the announcement had gone out in a different form from the one Richard felt he had agreed with Stan. I suggested four possibilities:

● Administrative error – unlikely but possible.

● 'Political decision' – Richard would indeed keep the UK for 12 months, but Stan chose not to say so in the announcement because it ran counter to the global/regional model.

● Communication problem – Stan did not think he had agreed what Richard thought he had.

● Back tracking – Stan had reneged on the agreement.

I stressed that Richard needed to understand which of these applied before confronting the issue. We agreed that clarification was the first objective of his meeting with Stan.

Assuming that it turned out to be a 'political' decision (which we both felt most likely), we examined what Richard's response should be. He could accept the status quo and go with the global product strategy role plus temporary responsibility for the UK – but in these circumstances he would have no real tenure of authority in the UK. His position was likely to be progressively undermined and we felt he would find it difficult to retain the confidence of his executive team and the UK workforce generally. We agreed that this was not the right approach.

We looked at his position six months after the take-over of Comsort.

How was he perceived by Jefferson? The short answer was that Jefferson needed him. In the short/medium term it was imperative for Stan to protect the UK revenue stream, which would have been the prime reason for Jefferson's acquisition of Comsort. In strategic terms, the UK was central to the European expansion programme and Richard, the key figure, would be difficult to replace. He recognized this and, though it was not in his nature to use threats to further his cause, did feel secure enough to take a firm line.

We discussed what that should be and agreed that one option was to seek to retain the joint role of VP, Global Product Strategy and Regional Manager, UK. But Richard was having renewed misgivings about the feasibility of this. Increasingly concerned by Jefferson's continuing failure to understand the distinct nature of the UK market, and recognizing that a global role would inevitably be time consuming, he feared the consequences of taking his eye off the UK. To compound this, Richard felt that his immediate team would be demoralized if they saw him dividing his allegiances, and was concerned that this could trigger departures. He would prefer simply to retain responsibility for the UK for a two-year period. We rehearsed the arguments he would use to support this approach.

Richard telephoned me on his return from the USA. Stan had finally agreed with the argument about the special nature of the UK market. Richard would be appointed Regional Manager, UK and would not, initially at least, take a global role. This volte-face came when Stan was persuaded to recognize the potentially disastrous consequences of diluting Richard's attention to the UK market. In the announcement no mention would be made of time scale, but it was agreed informally that the position would be reviewed after 12 months.

We used our next session to take stock of progress against the desired results established at the outset of the coaching programme. For his part Richard was positive, feeling that we were very much on target:

- The motivation of the Comsort management had been restored and many were beginning to look positively at new opportunities and challenges with Jefferson.

- It had been a difficult process, but Jefferson had come to realize that the UK was key to both components revenue and expansion strategy in Europe, and had agreed to treat it as a special case.

- Richard was now in a position to ensure that customers' requirements were met and their needs reflected in future product strategy.

- On the personal front, he had retained his general management responsibilities and avoided a work/lifestyle clash.

As far as Richard was concerned, the only significant negative was that, by opting for the UK role he had sacrificed the opportunity to contribute significantly to the strategy for continued European expansion.

I was less satisfied and shared with Richard my major concern. Our tactical approach was proving effective as far as it went. However, we were not getting to the core of the issue: did Jefferson have the right structure going forward to expand its components business in the UK and Continental Europe? Only by addressing this fundamental issue could Richard hope to achieve a lasting solution. By doing so he would also address his outstanding objective of strategic contribution.

As the coaching continued, we focused on the strategic issues of how to structure Jefferson for European expansion and persuade Stan to adopt a more radical approach by convincing him that the tried and tested Jefferson structure is no longer appropriate to the components business. We built the case for change carefully: the current structure of international divisions is used throughout Jefferson and has proved effective in the past; and Stan himself has little experience outside his homeland and would take some convincing that the US model is no longer the optimum.

Richard prepared a presentation for Stan using the Stopford and Wells 'International Structural Stages Model'. This drove home the point that Jefferson was employing a structure appropriate to low overseas sales and low product diversity while, following the Comsort acquisition, its overseas sales represent more than 50% of revenue and inject significant product diversity into the equation. He reiterated the fact that, to be successful in its bid for European expansion, Jefferson would need excellent local intelligence and an ability to respond rapidly and flexibly to local needs. It was unlikely to achieve this through global marketing, production and product strategy functions based in the USA. Bearing these factors in mind, it made sense to move to a regional structure with regional support functions.

On the interpersonal side, we spent more time on considering how Stan made his decisions and how best to influence him. While, as a leader, Richard concentrated on the details, Stan was a big picture man. To date, Richard had focused on tactical, short-term concerns around the existing UK business. This had been effective as far as it went, but would certainly not excite Stan's imagination. Richard focused on the far-reaching opportunities that developing the UK technology and customer base into Europe could afford for Jefferson.

In addition, Richard continued to work on:

- Achieving outstanding performance in the UK to show Stan that he was right to amend the structure to meet the differing needs of that market.

- Fostering the Comsort team's positive attitude towards their new owners and emphasizing career development possibilities.

- Encouraging cross-cultural relations, particularly by organizing working visits by Comsort managers to Jefferson's corporate headquarters and US plants.

- Monitoring recalcitrant Comsort staff and taking appropriate action.

- Adjusting the Comsort team's strategic thinking to embrace an international, rather than an insular UK, perspective.

Reaching a Resolution

To resolve the issues raised in this chapter, you need to consider the following questions:

● What is the new global agenda, and how can I address it?

● What national cultural issues do I need to consider and resolve, on both individual and corporate levels?

● How can we overcome the national perspectives and management biases within our own organization?

● Do we need to adapt our products/services or marketing strategies to meet local needs and the needs of a complex international organization?

● How can we use marketing to break down national preferences and prejudices?

● Do we have adequate PR in place to address the potential concerns of international pressure groups?

● Is our present structure the appropriate one to serve complex global operations?

● How can we create congruence between business, geographic and functional management requirements?

● How can I protect my work/life balance as the company becomes more international?

It's difficult to get a proper perspective when you're so close to the business – who can help with this piece?

Chapter 10

Balancing Your Act

Geoffrey Dale

Context

High on the agenda of every CEO is the need to achieve 'the right balance' – not only work/life balance, but also balance between what the job demands and what they bring to it. Working with CEOs on this task, I developed the idea of using a 'Personal Portfolio' (PP) to ensure that the individual's personal leadership agenda and focus as CEO remain relevant, clearly defined and properly balanced. The approach fits neatly with the 'Balanced Scorecard' concepts developed by Robert Kaplan and David Norton over the past 10 years.[1] Their work has shaped the vocabulary of business leaders and serves as a reminder of the importance of both *balance* and *measurement* in achieving professional success.

Widening the Balanced Scorecard approach to include work/life balance and blending this with the PP concept led me to the 'Balanced Personal Portfolio' (BPP), which covers both personal and professional goals. It has proved a powerful tool for CEOs and their organizations, increasing self-awareness and enhancing self-discipline, both individual and corporate, as well as providing guidance towards a more sensible and sustainable pattern of work and life at the top.

In the much the same way as the Balanced Scorecard added new dimensions to the traditional financial perspective (customers, processes and learning and growth), the BPP adds a personal dimension to the Balanced Scorecard, enabling the CEO to take a holistic view of his or her life. By embracing in one document both professional and personal lives, it shows very clearly how they both impact upon and complement each other.

Figure 10.1 shows the PP that I designed for the company which is focused on here. It gives an overview of the elements any PP should embrace.

So, how can a BPP help the CEO?

1. *Guidelines*	• How to get the most out of using the Personal Portfolios
2. *Personal Profile*	• Personal biographical information • Up-to-date profile within the firm and beyond
3. *Personal Portfolio Summary*	• A bullet point summary of the rest of the Portfolio • Planned allocation of time over year ahead • Key personal targets, contributions and accountabilities
4. *Client Work*	• Schedule of client work • Review of capacity and utilization
5. *Revenue Generation*	• Target billings • Schedule of projected and actual billings • Account management responsibilities
6. *Personal Development Plan*	• Career plan • Personal development plan for year ahead • Work/life balance plan
7. *Cost and Revenue Plan*	• Cost footprint within the firm • Support and resource requirements • Yield and profitability
8. *The Business Framework*	• Current-year business plan • Budget and monthly management information
9. *Review and Action*	• A personal 'Balance Scorecard' • A place to record review and action notes
10. *Other information for reference*	

Figure 10.1 *Personal portfolio – contents.*

It is the coach's ideal scenario to begin coaching CEOs on their appointment, and, potentially, a huge advantage for clients, who have a 'window of opportunity' as they enter their new roles. While it remains open, they have the chance to bring fresh perspectives to their tasks, define how to tackle the job, and identify their priorities and agenda. However, the window closes all too quickly! As the corporate grind takes over getting a proper perspective becomes much more difficult.

Much of my work with CEOs entails 're-opening' that window, using the BPP approach. Apart from the obvious benefits of fresh air to the overloaded brain, success enables CEOs to see their work and lives from a different angle. Having taken a deep breath and begun to appreciate the view, they can start building a robust and balanced approach to both the job and their lives as a whole. More importantly, they have learnt how to keep the window at least ajar for the future.

CEOs, and other top executives, may inherit job descriptions – often prepared as a basis for recruitment – but these are only starting points. A unique part of CEO's leadership task is:

- to define his or her own role
- to shape his or her approach within the role and define a personal contribution to the organization
- to continue to re-shape and re-define if necessary
- to ensure that it meets the requirements of the organization at each phase of its development

Critically, doing so can enable direct reports to shape their own contributions and define their PPs so that, individually and as a team, they address the main issues in a balanced and joined-up way.

I generally suggest that the client should develop a PP shaped to reflect his or her particular situation: to provide both a written statement of this agenda and a basis for monitoring progress towards defined goals. While the PP summary is no more than a couple of sheets of paper, it is no less powerful for being concise – bullet point statements resulting from a rigorous and comprehensive review of the approach to the job. Deeper detail is available in other parts of the PP.

While developing and maintaining a BPP hugely assists the CEO in disciplining a busy life, it can also be an invaluable tool for bottom-up forecasting when used across a company's top team. It will enable the CEO to see at a glance where the team's strengths and weaknesses lie; where development and recruitment are appropriate; what the people *can* do – and what they *want* to do. This last element is where the 'Personal' comes into Personal Portfolio.

As well as strictly business-related information, a *balanced* PP should allow for a statement of an individual's needs, for instance, to:

- decide that money is no longer the primary driver

- work part-time or from home

- combine paid work with voluntary work that 'gives something back'

- do work that plays to his or her knowledge, skills, values and experience

- continue personal learning and development

- maintain space for family, friends and interests.

It requires a more fundamental view of life, rather than just a statement of 'role objectives', which is important because the BPP is not a purely private document – it has to be shared with colleagues to be effective. This deeper understanding of what people want is not simply a 'nice to have'. For example: 'Jim' has written in his PP that he doesn't want to spend any time on generation this year, although it is one of his strengths and the company needs him to concentrate on this area. Jim's boss is forewarned that there will be negotiations ahead, and can prepare for them in advance. In contrast, 'Paul' wants to spend more time this year generating work, for which he has limited skills. The manager can plan his development and keep a close eye on his progress.

An additional benefit is that, when a team's PPs are public, colleagues will gain more rounded views of each other than are possible via 'water cooler' conversations, encouraging closer (therefore more productive and rewarding) relationships.

In the case of one client organization, where we were working with a rapidly growing consulting firm, we started by developing very comprehensive PPs to be used by each member of the team. Initially, the PP was a method of re-defining roles in a company whose structure was in the process of radical change. It soon became an invaluable tool for business forecasting. It also, in this particular case, served to protect the company's cherished collegiate ethos, since sharing personal aims and targets provides a solid foundation for teamwork.

The Client Company

Amorgos was founded in London in 1994 with a start-up team of four, to provide top-quality management consulting services working with people at or near board level. Established as a limited company it was run on a collegiate 'partnership' basis. Each consultant was both a partner and a director.

After five years there were 25 consultants with offices in London and throughout the UK. Steady year-on-year growth in revenue reflected a growing reputation and an impressive client list across a wide range of organizations and business sectors. Each of the partners received the same salary and bonus. They were still determined to avoid the bureaucracy most of them had experienced in other places, so formal structures were avoided. They were united by strongly shared values and behaviours that had proved more than 'nice-to-have features' of the firm, and were highly attractive to both clients and potential recruits.

The Client

Mohan had been one of the founders of Amorgos back in 1994. After qualifying as a chartered accountant with KPMG he moved to their consulting arm, where success led to partnership in 1981 and a quick succession of leadership roles, including running the Europe, Middle East, Africa Region (EMEA) as well as managing an impressive client list. In 1994 he focused on his core value of collegiality in management consulting and founded Amorgos. He and his wife, a solicitor, have three children aged 13, 19 and 21. Mohan spends much of his free time involved in charitable work in the wider community. He chairs a network for senior ethnic minority executives and writes regularly for *Management Consulting* journal.

The Challenge

By 1999, the challenge for Amorgos was how to sustain its rapid growth without destroying its unique ethos, which clients saw as a vital differentiator and a prime source of the value created for them. Mohan and his colleagues recognized the need to provide a robust business framework within which the consulting team could operate. At a series of Away Days, which I had facilitated, a clear business strategy had been developed, Mohan appointed as CEO, and an executive group of four appointed to manage day-to-day business operations within the agreed framework.

Although a founder of the firm, Mohan had until now been a peer of his colleagues, and realized that there might be opposition to this structural change. Nonetheless, at this point the firm required a single leader: a figurehead, an overall decision maker and a defined place where the buck stopped. Mohan needed to bring authority to the CEO role without damaging his good relationships with the team. He had always worked in a relatively informal and egalitarian way. Now he needed to develop into his new role in ways consistent with the strong culture of the firm as well as with his own personality, philosophy and personal needs.

Mohan had also been very much hands-on in all areas of the business, including financial control and operational management. He would not have time for this level of involvement from now on, and had to learn to stand back. At the same time he had been a major generator of revenue and of new accounts, which he managed personally with great success, delivering much of the work himself as well as providing work for colleagues. In appointing him CEO the firm was potentially 'losing' his significant fee-earning capability, so it was essential to find a way to fill this gap.

The Desired Results

● To develop Personal Portfolios for all 25 consultants and use them for bottom-up business forecasting and management.

● To ensure that plans are in place to meet generation and delivery targets.

● To create an effective method of managing the growing business, while harnessing the diversity of the team and maintaining an acceptable work/life balance.

● To use Personal Portfolios to monitor individual performance, encouraging a disciplined, self-managed approach.

● To retain the unique and valuable culture of Amorgos.

The Developing Approach

My initial sessions with Mohan had revolved around the re-structuring of Amorgos and the defining of the company's aims and business strategy. Now the new structure was in place, we needed to deal with the specific issue of maintaining growth while protecting the Amorgos culture. Mohan and I agreed that I should work in parallel with him and his team over the next year. We would have regular one-to-one meetings and I would provide wider support by working with him to design and facilitate Away Days for the whole consulting team. Where appropriate, I would involve my Change Partnership colleagues to support the process.

My first thought was that the PP would be the ideal tool for managing this group of 'self-managing' and very independent consultants in a consultative fashion which would minimize any resentment caused by Mohan's 'promotion'. Mohan and the executive group would be able to take each individual's personal 'wants' into consideration, define and use his or her gifts, and monitor progress in an appropriately collegiate way.

In addition, sharing the PP information among all consultants – at regular plenary discussions and by having them on the firm's database for reference – would protect, and potentially enhance, Amorgos' close partnership ethos. It would allow the team to play to each member's particular strengths and interests, while having clarity about individual accountability within a clearly understood business framework. The emphasis would be on providing a disciplined but self-managed approach and avoiding unnecessary bureaucracy.

We shall see how the PP evolved at Amorgos in a moment but it may be helpful at this point to look briefly at the process that was developed.

From the start at Amorgos the concept was developed as a physical portfolio – an A4 size D-ring binder with a 10-part divider to help organize the contents. Although much of the content was available on the computer system it was found that having hard-copy versions in a common framework for reference was helpful for individual consultants in managing their own portfolios. It also proved useful in working with other members of the team. The contents page of the original Amorgos portfolio is shown in Figure 10.1.

The titles of the individual sections speak for themselves. The crucial documents are:

Section 3: Personal Portfolio Summary, which gives an overview of:

- targets (including those for *Client Work* and *Revenue Generation*)

- projected earnings and expected costs

- membership of the executive group, where appropriate

- individual accountabilities for areas like marketing, account management, supervision, professional development and research and development

- contributions in a wide range of areas that reflected the individual's particular interest or aptitude.

And Section 6, Personal Development Plan which includes:

- work-related development plans

- the individual's preferences in terms of work

- personal information that builds a picture of the whole individual and how his or her ideal work/life balance might be achieved

Other parts of the PP will provide the detail behind the summary for purposes of performance management. These detailed sections will give essential information for regular reviews, and necessary *ad hoc* performance checks.

I explained the PP concept to Mohan and worked on his current PP summary (as a peer within the team) with him. I asked him to sketch out a revised summary (as CEO) for our next session, at which we would review and complete it. We would share the revised summary with the other 24 consultants at our first away day in order to demonstrate the process. Figures 10.2 and 10.3 show Mohan's summaries.

Key dimensions	Plan	Actual/notes
1. Time: Availability and Allocation		
• Total available days (full-time = 222)	222	
• Total available hours (total days × 9)	2000	
• Planned hours on delivering MC work	1100	
• Planned hours on revenue generation	700	
• Planned hours on personal development	20	
• Planned hours on business development and other activities	180	Internal meetings, preparation, PR work, etc.
2. Client Work Delivery Plan		
• Planned hours for MC work	1000	Supervising five consulting projects
• Planned hours on other client work	100	Running one workshop
• Target value of work delivered (£)	£700 k	
3. Revenue Generation Plan		
• Target Project Wins:	10	Winning 10 projects
– Value	£1.2 m	
– Target billings	£1.2 m	
4. Personal Development Plan		
– Budget	£1000	Conference attendance
– PDP goal: Build high level networks over year		
– Charitable commitments take 6 days a year and 12 evenings		
– Ethnic Minorities Network commitments take 12 days a year and 24 evenings		
– Holidays + time to spend with family (6 weeks and weekends)		
– Writing for *MC* journal takes 12 days per year		
– Golf 24 days per year!		
5. Cost and Resource Plan		
• Personal direct costs	£100,000	Salary
• Travel/expenses – Estimate	£7000	
• Support costs – Average days/week	5	
– Estimated cost	£30,000	PA
• Other client related costs	£3000	Client entertainment, etc.
• PDP costs	£1000	
• Overhead allocation	£5000	Office, computers, phone etc
• Total costs p.a.	£146,000	
6. Other specific Roles and Accountabilities		
• Producing management accounts		
• Coaching new colleagues in selling techniques		
• Day-to-day operational business management		

Figure 10.2 *Personal Portfolio summary for Mohan before appointment as CEO.*

Key Dimensions	Plan	Actual/Notes
1. Time: Availability and Allocation		
• Total available days (Full-time = 222)	222	
• Total available hours (total days × 9)	2000	
• Planned hours on delivering work	150	Overseeing one crucial project
• Planned hours on revenue generation	0	
• Planned hours on personal development	30	Senior executive coaching
• Planned hours on leading and managing Amorgos	1820	Board meetings, PR and press, managing business, recruitment and planning staff development
2. Client Work Delivery Plan		
• Planned hours for delivery of consulting work	150	
• Planned hours on other client work	0	
• Target value of work delivered (£)	£100k	
3. Revenue Generation Plan		
• Target New Business: Number projects	0	
– Value	0	
– Target billings	0	
4. Personal Development Plan		
– Budget	£17,000	Senior executive coaching
– PDP: Build high level networks and leading Amorgos into more growth		
– Unwilling to renege on charitable commitments		
– Have agreed to speak at a conference on ethnic diversity York in May		
– Network management is great for building strong high level networks while giving back to the community		
– Need time in July for son's graduation from university		
– Want to take all of my allocated 6 weeks holiday; didn't last year and this has an impact on everyone around me!		
– Journal writing boosts company profile, so important		
5. Cost and Resource Plan		
• Personal direct costs	£200,000	Salary
• Travel/Expenses – Estimate	£17,000	
• Support costs – Average days/week	5	
– Estimated cost	£35,000	PA
• Other client related costs	£7,000	Client entertainment, etc.
• PDP costs	£17,000	
• Overhead allocation	£8,000	Office, computers, phone, etc.
• Total costs p.a.	£254,000	
6. Other Specific Roles and Accountabilities		
• Plan long-term strategy for business and communicate to all stakeholders		
• Manage the business and the people in Amorgos		
• Scout mergers and acquisitions opportunities (and negotiate deals)		
• Represent Amorgos in the financial community, to the press, etc.		

Figure 10.3 *Personal Portfolio summary for Mohan after appointment as CEO.*

The most striking difference between the two summaries was that, with his new CEO duties taking precedence, Mohan would certainly not be able to generate £1.2 million-worth of business, or deliver £700,000-worth of work, as he had done in the previous year. Other members of the team would need to make up this drop, or new consultants would need to be recruited. It was also important to Mohan that he should continue with his charitable work and ethnic minority work, and that he should be able to protect his relationships with his wife and children from the rigours of his new corporate role.

Mohan's personal needs raised the question of 'How much is enough money?' The original Amorgos consultants had begun their business with a very clear understanding that money was not their main motivator. This is why all were partners and directors, and why they were all paid the same salaries and bonuses. They all wanted high salaries and were prepared to work hard for them, but there was a limit to how much they wanted – or expected to be asked – to sacrifice for profit. Most had left 'big five' firms for this very reason. The company's enormous growth over the past five years had been managed without damage to this element of their culture, and each new consultant joined on the same basis as the original four.

I facilitated an Away Day six weeks after Mohan's appointment as CEO. Having an external facilitator enabled Mohan to participate fully in the event as a team member. Using a mix of plenary sessions and breakouts, and with a lot of good work done during coffee breaks and over lunch and dinner, we worked our way through our agenda.

Since the Amorgos culture was at the forefront of the participants' minds, I began by helping them to 'map' that culture. They defined, in three concise documents, the company's:

● core purpose

● values

● behaviours (expressing those values).

An important question still remained, how could this new structure be embedded without damage to the unique collegiate ethos?

Some of the team thought that a changed culture was inevitable, given the company's expected growth over the coming year, and argued for a much more 'hard-edged' approach with much clearer accountability for performance, definition of roles, individual targets and closer monitoring of performance. Others felt that the unique features of the firm were non-negotiable. Could these conflicting views be reconciled? We would only be able to answer this question retrospectively. Given the company's new structure and projected growth, it would take practical measures as well as good intentions to balance the two viewpoints. At this point we introduced the PP concept as a practical measure, shared Mohan's revised PP Summary with the rest of the consultants, and explained the theory behind it, which I summarized as:

● insight from Balanced Scorecard concepts

● how the Balanced Personal Portfolio was different, and might be a way for the larger team to continue to operate on a self-managed basis, but in a disciplined way which would ensure that the consultants' combined contributions met the needs of the business as well as their personal needs.

Mohan then aired his concerns about the potential gap in generation and delivery caused by his change of role and his desire to work out as a team how to cover that gap.

It was agreed that all the other consultants would create PPs before our next meeting, which would be shared so we could forecast for the business in a collegiate way. We decided to include the core documents on purpose, values and behaviours that we had created earlier in the introduction to the PPs, to provide important context.

In preparation for the next meeting I worked with an Amorgos volunteer, and consulted informally with others, to develop a format for the company's specific PPs. I also had one-to-one meetings with other members of the team – eight consultants who between them, in Mohan's view, represented the range of views on how the business needed to move forward. I guided them through working on the BPPs, and used my discussions with them to gain an understanding of what sticky issues might arise.

I then designed a one-day event to enable the whole consulting team to address the questions arising which reflected closely the issues Mohan had flagged up in our early meetings.

That meeting began with a chart on the wall titled 'What Does Amorgos Need?', which had been created by Mohan and the executive group.

There were also two blank flip-charts on view, titled 'What Can I Contribute?' and 'What Do I Want to Contribute?' We explained that these would be filled in as the consultants revealed the contents of their PP summaries.

We then went round the table, as every consultant read out and explained his PP summary. When all had been shared, and the empty flip-charts filled in we had three charts – see Figure 10.4.

There were some glaring differences between the company's needs and the consultants' capabilities and desires, which necessitated discussion and negotiation. We broke for lunch, for which I had allowed two hours, so that the consultants would be able to talk about the morning's work and begin thinking about the coming negotiation in an informal social setting.

In the afternoon the negotiation achieved the following results.

Business Generation – Target £5 million

- Mohan agreed to continue with generation for the next six months while other consultants were developed to cover his revenue.

- Mark, Kevin and Leila committed themselves to bringing in £600,000 each.

- The rest of the committed to bringing in £3.2 million between them, in identified tranches

- Andrew, Alex, Sarah and Jaime, four of the best business generators, agreed to mentor and develop the generation skills of Clare, Miles, Wei and John, who wanted to learn more about this. (Mohan and I took note of the people who committed to business generation reluctantly, in anticipation of potential performance and motivational issues.)

Delivery – Target £5 million

- Andrew, Alex, Sarah and Jaime would be doing less delivery, which would reduce it to £5m again (from the projected £5.9m).

Restructure

- Everything is on course.

- They agreed that a sub-group should be assembled to embed the new structure.

Continuing Professional Development

- Cameron, Liz and Walter agree to put their book collaboration off and concentrate on business generation instead.

- Kirsten and Suresh are encouraged to write articles in business journals. The other three agree to spend the time on generation.

- Ten people can go on one conference each over the coming year (10 conferences).

- Mohan and the executive team can go for senior executive coaching (five people).

- Ten people can take one internal training courses each. (Ten courses.) Four of the requested courses were on generation. They will now receive the equivalent from top generators, as described above.

What does Amorgos need?	What can I contribute?	What do I want to contribute?
Generation: £5 million • Others to cover Mohan's £1.2m	*Generation – £4.8 million* • Mark, Kevin and Leila can bring in £600,000 each. • The rest of the group can bring in £3 million between them. • There would be a £0.2 million shortfall from the generation target. This needs to be discussed and resolved! • The group as a whole could, if stretched, generate up to £6	*Generation – £3.5 million* • Mark, Kevin and Leila want to bring in £600,000 each. The rest of the group to bring in £1.7 million between wants them. • There would be a £1.5 million shortfall from the generation target.
Delivery: £5 million • Others to cover Mohan's £600,000	*Delivery – £5.9 million* • Alex, Rob and Sonia can deliver £350,000 each. The rest of the group can deliver £4.9 million between them. • This would be £900,000 over generation targets. • More people need to be encouraged away from delivery into generating business.	*Delivery – £6.5 million* • Alex, Rob and Sonia want to deliver £300,000 each. The rest of the group wants to deliver £5.6 million between them. • This would be £1.5m over generation targets. • Clearly, this team prefers delivery to generation!
Restructure • Mohan will spend 75% of his time managing the business and growing it through M&A. • Executive team of four will spend 20% of their time collectively managing ops	*Restructure* • Mohan can spend 75% of his time managing the business and growing it through M&A. • Executive team of four can spend 20% of their time collectively managing ops	*Restructure* • Mohan wants to spend 75% of his time managing the business and growing it through M&A. • Executive Team of four wants to spend 20% of their time collectively managing ops
Continuing Professional Development • Continuing personal development of all partners	*Continuing Professional Development* • Cameron, Liz and Walter have been invited to collaborate on a book	*Continuing Professional Development* • Three people want to collaborate on a book • Nine people want to contribute articles to

- Must be kept to a minimum
- Maximum costs £4m

Collegiate ethos must be retained
- Mohan must manage his new role as CEO without creating resentment
- The Executive Group must perform their duties with minimum bureaucracy and officiousness
- Respect for diversity in team. Acknowledge that different contributions are equally valuable. Allow working from home, part-time, etc.
- We must ensure that Amorgos remains a fun place to work

- Tom, Kirsten, Suresh, Clive and Janie have been asked to write articles for business journals
- There are 10 people who would benefit from attending conferences
- Five people are appropriate candidates for Senior Executive Coaching
- Twelve people would benefit from taking internal courses

Costs
- The company wants costs of £4m max
- Projected costs allowing for the consultants' 'wants' above are £4.8m
- Costs can be held to £4 million, but not if all the wants are allowed

Collegiate ethos must be retained
- A collegiate approach could be fostered by creating and sharing Personal Portfolios, and using them for bottom-up forecasting and management
- Some consultants could work part-time
- Some consultants could work from home sometimes
- Everyone should retain respect for diversity within the team
- The company should continue being a fun place to work

- business journals
- Ten people want to go on four conferences each over the coming year (40 conferences!)
- Eight people want to go for senior executive coaching
- Twelve people want to take three internal training courses each (30 courses)

Costs
- The company wants costs of £4 million maximum

Collegiate ethos must be retained
- The group as a whole wants to use the Personal Portfolio approach
- Eight people want to work part-time
- 20 people want to work from home sometimes
- Everyone wants to retain respect for diversity within the team
- Everyone wants the company to continue being a fun place to work
- Jessica wants to take time off to do a charity climb of Kilimanjaro
- William needs to take time off for surgery
- Rachel will be taking maternity leave this year

Figure 10.4 *What does Amorgos Need?*

Collegiate Ethos Must be Retained

- Eight people will be allowed to work part-time.

- Twenty people will be allowed to work from home sometimes.

- Everyone will retain respect for diversity within the team and agree that different contributions are equally valuable.

- The team as a whole has always enjoyed socializing both informally after hours and at family-included day treats (Ascot, Wimbledon, Alton Towers) and weekends (partners' meetings combined with trips to Le Touquet, Madrid, Disney World). It is agreed that they will continue to fund and make time for events like this, which make Amorgos a fun place to work.

- Jessica will be allowed to take paid time off to do a charity climb of Kilimanjaro.

- Colleagues agree to cover William's surgery and recuperation time.

- Mike, Toby, Phil and Janie will cover Rachel's work while she is on maternity leave.

Costs Must Be Kept to a Minimum

- The company wants to set a ceiling on costs of £4 million.

- Projected costs allowing for the consultants' unfettered 'wants' were £4.8 million.

- But, after negotiation on the 'wants', costs will be held to £4 million.

These negotiations were sometimes heated but always respectful. Although he had not previously mentioned it, Mohan wanted an increase of £1.1 million in business generation, to cover a 30% increase in bonuses and the recruitment of four new people, to enable a new phase of expansion. He now revealed this and stepped into the leadership role by painting his vision for growth in some detail. After discussion, the group agreed that this target would mean longer hours and more time away from home. Since the majority had families and/or out-of-work interests that would make these changes undesirable, they agreed to forego bigger bonuses, yet still committed to a £600,000 increase in generation to cover the costs of the four additional consultants. I had expected this negotiation to be fraught with resentment, but the strong Amorgos culture had clearly led to the recruitment of remarkably like-minded people who would work harder to improve their business, but felt that they already earned enough and wanted time to enjoy it!

For three years now, Amorgos has developed its annual revenue budget on the basis of 'bottom-up' proposals from individuals consultants. This is a direct spin-off from the PP approach. There is considerable variation between the revenue targets across the team, reflecting the differentiation between consultants' overall contributions: some being major revenue generators, others happy to focus on delivering work with clients, with more modest revenue targets. There is recognition, too, of other ways in which members of the team contribute to the business. Managing this diversity was one of Mohan's priorities and the development of a Balanced Personal Scorecard within the PP was a direct response to this need.

From the summaries and personal development plans, Mohan and the executive group can now 'manage' the other consultants in a way that is aligned with the Amorgos ethos, taking into account personal needs, the value of 'gifts differing' and the company's requirements. Each consultant edits his own PP annually and the results are collated into the overarching Amorgos portfolio for the following year. Quarterly or half-yearly review meetings are held with the individuals according to need, and the entire group meets half-yearly. Thus contributions and progress are monitored individually and collectively. All of this is shared.

For Mohan, the structure and format of the BPP developed for Amorgos was driven by pure logic, combined with his passionate

belief in the principles and values which had shaped the development of the business. Amorgos was a people business, so he began
by recognizing that:

- The different gifts and interests within the team do not need to
  conform to a pattern – indeed, they are richer if they do not –
  though they must make sense within the agreed business framework.

- The dynamic process evolves as people grow, develop and
  demonstrate new ways of contributing.

- Delivering outstanding work with clients is the prime focus, but
  beyond this, each consultant must make a unique 'own contribution', according to individual strengths and interests, but
  always within a clear business framework.

Revenue generation was crucial, but some degree of speculation was
now required. In developing the team Mohan realized that there
would be some natural big revenue generators and others who
would be more effective focusing on delivering work with clients –
perhaps with quite modest new business generation targets. The
revenue generation section of the portfolio was not a vehicle for
imposing unrealistic revenue targets on unwilling colleagues, but
a way of managing this diversity.

Mohan and his colleagues can now ensure that the different
contributions of each member of the team not only add up to
meet the needs and aspirations of the business, but also represent
a balanced and fair contribution. The open and continuous process
of self-assessment, supported by review with colleagues, has
demonstrated that it can meet the needs of individuals for effective
feedback and, where appropriate enable the firm to deal with
situations where individual contributions do not match up to
the needs of the business. The logic was completed in Mohan's
mind by the section headed *Cost and Resource Plan* – a basis
for looking at the yield and 'profitability' of the individuals
contribution.

When all this is brought together in the annual budget it is easy to recognize that the combined efforts of the whole team are greater than the sum of the parts – that they can achieve things together which would not be possible on their own. In fact, focusing on this has provided an important spin-off of the PP – identifying the processes within the business which really 'create value' for clients and thus for all the shareholders in the business.

All this has been achieved without damage to the Amorgos culture.

On a personal level, the BPP discipline has made it part of Mohan's routine to define and consider his personal needs in advance. Thus, and by making that detail available to all consultants and staff, he has ensured that he can protect the time he spends with his family and on outside interests that are important to him.

The other consultants have found that the BPP approach has enabled each of them to develop his own unique approach to his work, role and contribution, and yet still achieve demanding business targets. Rather than operating in a straitjacket of top-down directives and targets, it allows the team members to explore their individual creativity, and to direct their energies in ways – and into areas – which suit them as discrete individuals. This has released powerful energies within the business, and is these which have helped to drive Amorgos' 40%+ per year growth rates in recent times.

It is important, however, to stress that the approach outlined above, and the particular format of the PP created for Amorgos, were specific to the needs of that business at a particular phase in its development. It is not set in stone. It has been adapted and refined to ensure it remains relevant and helpful. The concept can be adapted for any business but should not be slavishly followed.

Reaching a Resolution

To develop and use the PP approach effectively you should:

- Define your priorities to shape your overall contribution and balance your PP to meet the needs of the organization.

- Realize that maintaining a BPP is not a soft option but a leadership imperative.

- Recognize individual strengths and weaknesses in yourself and your team so you can empower every member to develop and play to his or her strengths and make his or her unique contributions.

- Acknowledge each team member's individual contribution. This will release new energy, increase motivation and give people a real sense of ownership of the shared objectives.

- Focus on the key value drivers in the organization and shape priorities and personal agendas to deliver measurable outcomes. Everybody from CEO down will then be able to see how his or her contribution 'makes a difference'.

- Foster across the team the sense of being more in control of one's job and life. This generates positive, pro-active approaches which can transform individual and corporate performance.

- Ensure that the PPs are reviewed in a systematic way. This helps achieve that crucial balance between the needs of the organization, the individual and the team.

Aaaah, help at last!

Conclusion

Peter Milligan

Sleepless nights are a sign of stress. This stress can be caused by the myth that the CEO must be a god-like figure, all-knowing and all-powerful. Fortunately, this myth is losing currency and another view of leadership is emerging to replace it.

This book has given 10 examples of individuals and organizations developing in some way. In each situation, the CEO, guided by his or her coach, has tapped into the intelligence within and around him or her to find better ways to achieve a desired outcome. Its aim is to illustrate how any CEO can use the techniques of the coach to resolve a range of problems and become a more effective leader.

Ten Keys to Effective Leadership

There is no single formula for being great and inspiring others to greatness. However, the following characteristics and capabilities have emerged throughout the book as interrelated and essential to effective leadership.

Consciousness

A fundamental characteristic of effective leaders is being 'awake' – not only to what is going on inside themselves, but also to what is going on in their people, their organization and the world beyond. This wakefulness is not the same as stress-induced insomnia!

Congruence

The word congruent means 'aligned' or 'in agreement.' When there is *real* congruence in an organization there is true agreement on its values, purpose and objectives. Everyone's words *and* actions demonstrate a shared vision and commitment that extends beyond what they say and do to include what they truly think and feel. The power of this should never be underestimated.

Real congruence begins with the leader. Leaders who truly 'walk the talk' begin to win the trust and respect of those around them. They demonstrate integrity as they seek to correct, rather than simply cover up, mistakes. They embody the principles they espouse and know that alignment is less stressful and more effective in the long run. Essentially, their 'doing' is aligned with their 'being' and somehow this seems to inspire others to do likewise.

Compassion

The January 2002 *Harvard Business Review* featured an article entitled 'Leading in Times of Trauma'.[1] Among its examples it cites the different responses of business leaders to the 11 September terrorist attacks. The CEOs who immediately focused on the emotional needs of the staff and their families, accelerated the healing process and found loyalty actually increasing in their work-forces. In contrast, those who showed no compassion, expecting people to turn up to work as if nothing had happened, quickly lost the respect, loyalty and commitment of their staff. The impact of the different approaches is striking and instructive for all leaders.

Connection

A sense of connection is vital to the well-being of individuals and organizations. Sustainable success comes to those who recognize the truth in Martin Luther King's statement that we are all 'caught in an inescapable network of mutuality, tied in a single garment of destiny'. Connection must be felt both within and beyond organizational boundaries.

Internally, great teamwork emerges when people feel connected to each other through a shared sense of purpose. When the sense of connection extends to the impact of what the organization does and how it does it, corporate objectives are likely to be supported even more widely. Business leaders can no longer afford to see 'doing well' and 'doing good' as incompatible. A growing focus on the 'triple bottom line' means that companies must not only strive to be profitable, but also be cognizant of social and environmental responsibility. SRI (socially responsible investment) is not a fad, but a structural trend – it is increasingly difficult to sustain a business that makes money by damaging people, communities or nature.

Communication

Many leaders believe that communication is simply about 'telling' people things. It is not, however, possible to sustain influence without finding common ground on which relationships can be built. True communication requires intelligent listening as well as speaking. Employees, customers and other stakeholders expect to be heard, not just talked at. Ignoring this fact comes at a high price. Talented knowledge workers, insulted by a command and control style of management, will take their talent and knowledge elsewhere. Customers, increasingly aware of corporate propaganda, will also desert the organization if they don't feel their needs are being adequately considered. Trying to manage perception through presentation is not sufficient. Influence comes with having, and showing, a good understanding of your audience.

Culture

In her book *Leadership and the New Science* Margaret Wheatley[2] writes about the invisible fields that shape behaviour: 'To learn what's in the field, look at what people are doing. They have picked up the messages, discerned what is truly valued, and then shaped their behaviour accordingly.'

Organizational effectiveness depends heavily on having a culture that reflects true alignment of purpose and engenders trust in participants and stakeholders. Culture is also becoming an increasingly important factor in the attraction and retention of talent. An essential part of the leader's role, therefore, is being able to create and sustain this powerful invisible field to produce positive outcomes. Effective leaders shape culture through personal congruence, communication skills and the courage of their convictions.

Courage

All great human endeavour features acts of courage. Often associated with great leadership, it is a quality that opens up new possibilities for the courageous person and those around them.

In an article in the *Financial Times*,[3] Professor Adrian Furnham named three types of courage essential in a business leader: the courage to take risks, the courage to confront and moral courage.

The CEO needs all three.

A CEO must overcome the fear of failure. Calculating risk is important, but leading is about being first – and being brave enough to take responsibility for failure if it comes. A CEO must also recognize that pussyfooting around difficult issues does no one any favours in the long term. Reluctance to deal with raw emotion is one of the main reasons why appraisal systems fail. A good leader can muster the courage to speak honestly (but not brutally), and thoughtfully (with compassion), and must be prepared to stand by a set of principles even when it might seem easier to compromise them in the name of personal or corporate gain.

Courageous leaders are better able to inspire and 'en*courage*' others towards the development of an enterprising culture where people are willing to take risks and responsibility. They know that courage reflects confidence, and also builds it.

Confidence

Leaders who lack confidence in themselves and others will tend to panic at setbacks, precipitately change course and give the impression of inconsistency or, worse, indecision. In this state they are also more likely to blame circumstances and other people for problems.

Effective leaders understand that confidence is the foundation that supports competence. Recognizing the power of self-confidence, they continually seek to build it in themselves *and* the people on whom they depend. While not afraid to confront problems, they also constantly look for opportunities to acknowledge success. This inspires confidence and the motivation to take on new challenges. It is the best way to develop an energetic and resilient team.

Creativity

It could be said that creativity occurs on the boundary of chaos and order. Revolutionary ideas and behaviours must be balanced with some structure and stability for the creative process to be complete. Good leaders ensure the sustained success of their organizations by being able to move people between these two worlds. Turbulent times will require them to provide a sense of order and meaning so that people can transform the uncertainty and difficulties into something positive. On the other hand, when things are stable, they are willing to unsettle people by challenging the prevailing paradigm.

The futurist Daniel Burrus[4] says to companies, 'kill your cash cow'. That would seem insane to anyone focused purely on short-term financial performance, but what he means is that organizations need to constantly reinvent and renew themselves, and to think ahead – because today's cash cow may end up being tomorrow's dead horse!

Coaching Style

Coaching should not simply be the domain of the full-time professional coach. A good leader seeks to bring the best out of others by developing and refining a 'coaching style' in his or her day-to-day work with them. More than just a set of techniques, truly powerful coaching reflects an *underlying attitude* towards people. A coaching style shows respect for people, and recognizes their ability and potential. Coaching is about 'education' in the original sense of the word: it is about asking the right questions to 'lead out' the inherent wisdom that can be found in all people when they are supported to contribute, learn and grow.

The leader whose people walk away from each interaction with him or her feeling more conscious, more cared about, and more confident in their capacity to succeed, will enjoy an easier and more fulfilling life than the leader who is unable to inspire and challenge in this way.

A recent report, 'Developing Business Leaders for 2010'[5] highlights the escalating challenges ahead and the fact that many future executives may be either unable or unwilling take on demanding top executive positions. The effective leader, it says, will have little choice but to build and unleash teams.

Sustained success comes to the CEO able to develop the 'invisible field' that productively shapes the thinking and behaviour of individuals and teams in and around the organization. Rather than regarding themself as the source of power and knowledge, he or she regards themself as an agent whose personal congruence and communication skills will align and develop people in order to release the potential of the organization. The CEO who does this will sleep much more soundly at night.

Notes and References

Introduction

1. Research conducted by Hay among Standard & Poor's 500 companies.
2. Spencer Stuart's 2001 UK board Index of the top 150 companies.

Chapter 1

1. Covey, S.R., Merrill, Roger A., Merrill, Rebecca R., *First Thing First*, 1993, Simon & Schuster.
2. Fritz, Robert, *Creating*, 1993, Ballantine Books.
3. Landsberg, Max, *The Tools of Leadership*, 2000, HarperCollins Business.
4. Herb, Leslie, Price, *McKinsey Quarterly*, 2001 Number 2.

Chapter 3

1. Covey, Stephen R., *The Seven Habits of Highly Effective People*, 1989, Simon & Schuster.
2. Gallwey, Timothy, *The Inner Game of Work*, 2002, Texere.

Chapter 5

1. *Daily Telegraph*, March 1996.
2. Collins J.C. and Porras, J.I., *Built to Last, Successful Habits of Visionary Companies*, 1994, 1997, HarperCollins, New York.
3. Ghoshal, S. and Bartlett, C.A., *The Individualized Corporation, A Fundamentally New Approach to Management*, 1997, HarperCollins, New York.
4. Godfrey, S., *An Inquiry into the Links Between Personal Renewal and Corporate Transformation*, 2000, University of Surrey.

Chapter 8

1. Hofstede, Geert, *Cultures and Organizations: Software of the Mind*, 1991, McGraw-Hill.
2. Trompenaar, Fons and Hampden-Turner, Charles, *Riding the Waves of Culture: Understanding Cultural Diversity in Business*, 1997, Nicholas Brealey.
3. Cox Jnr., Taylor, *Developing Competency to Manage Diversity*, 1997, Berrett-Koehler.
4. Schneider-Ross, *Moving On Up?*, 1999–2000, Runnymede Trust.
5. Coffey, E., Huffington, C., Thomson, P., *The Changing Culture of Leadership – Women Leaders' Voices*, 1999, The Change Partnership.
6. Recruiting, Retaining and Progressing the Careers of Minority Ethnic Staff in the Probation Service, July 2000.

Chapter 9

1. Stopford, J. M. and Wells Jnr., L. T., *Managing the Multinational Enterprise*, 1972, New York Basic Books.
2. Bartlett, Christopher A. and Ghoshal, Sumantra, *Managing Across Borders – The Transnational Solution*, 1989, Hutchinson.

Chapter 10

1. Kaplan, Robert S. and Norton, David P., *Having Trouble With Your Strategy? Then Map It*, September 2000, Harvard Business School Press.

Conclusion

1. Wheatley, Margaret J., *Leadership and the New Science*, 1999, Berrett-Koehler.
2. Furnham, Professor Adrian, *Industry Needs More Captains Courageous*, from The Financial Times, 5 September 2001.
3. Burrus, David, *Technotrends: How to Use Your Technology To Go Beyond Your Competition*, 1993, Harper Business.
4. The Conference Board, *Developing Business Leaders for 2010*, 3 May 2002.

Bibliography

Bartlett, Christopher A. and Ghoshal, Sumantra, *Managing Across Borders – The Transnational Solution*, 1989, Hutchinson Business Books.

Burrus, David, *Technotrends: How to Use Your Technology To Go Beyond Your Competition*, 1993, Harper Business.

Coffey, Elizabeth; Huffington, Clare; Thomson, Peninah, *The Changing Culture of Leadership – Women Leaders' Voices*, 1999, The Change Partnership.

Collins J. C. and Porras, J. I., *Built to Last, Successful Habits of Visionary Companies*, 1994, 1997, Harper Collins, New York.

Covey, S. R., Merril, Roger A., Merrill, Rebecca R., *First Thing First*, 1993, Simon & Schuster.

Covey, Stephen R., *The Seven Habits of Highly Effective People*, 1989, Simon & Schuster.

Cox Jnr., Taylor, *Developing Competency to Manage Diversity*, 1997, Berrett-Koehler Publishers Inc.

Fritz, Robert, *Creating*, 1993, Ballantine Books.

Furnham, Professor Adrian, *Industry Needs More Captains Courageous*, from The Financial Times, 5 September 2001.

Gallwey, Timothy, *The Inner Game of Work*, 2000, Orion Business Books.

Ghoshal, S. and Bartlett, C. A., *The Individualized Corporation, A Fundamentally New Approach to Management*, 1997, Harper Collins, New York.

Godfrey, S., *An Inquiry into the Links Between Personal Renewal and Corporate Transformation*, 2000, University of Surrey.

Hofstede, Geert, *Cultures and Organizations: Software of the Mind*, 1991, McGraw-Hill Book Company, Europe.

Kaplan, Robert S. and Norton, David P., *Having Trouble With Your Strategy? Then Map It*, September 2000, Harvard Business School Press.

Landsberg, Max, *The Tools of Leadership*, 2000, Harper Collins Business.

Lilius, Jacoba M., Dutton, Jane E., Frost, Peter, Worline, Monica C., Kanov, Jason M., Leading in Times of Trauma, January 2002, *Harvard Business Review*.

Probation Service: Recruiting, Retaining and Progressing the Careers of Minority Ethnic Staff in the Probation Service, July 2000.

Schneider-Ross, *Moving On Up?*, 1999-2000, Runnymede Trust.

Spencer Stuart's 2001 UK board Index of the top 150 companies.

Stopford, J. M. and Wells Jnr., L. T., *Managing the Multinational Enterprise*, 1972, New York Basic Books.

The Conference Board, *Developing Business Leaders for 2010*, 3 May 2002.

Trompenaar, Fons and Hampden-Turner, Charles, *Riding the Waves of Culture: Understanding Cultural Diversity in Business*, 1997, Nicholas Brealey Publishing Limited.

Wheatley, Margaret J., *Leadership and the New Science*, 1999, Berrett-Koehler Publishers.

Index